MW00843353

How to Make & Repair
Leather Doll Bodies

By LaVonne Lutterman

Publisher
Gregory Bayer

Editor
Kim Shields

Production Team
Jean Adams
Cindy Boutwell
Cindy McCarville

Cover Design
Rebecca Haas

Cover Materials
Jan Tessen
LaVonne Lutterman

Cover Photo
Mary Kay Berg

Jones Publishing, Incorporated
N7450 Aanstad Road
P.O. Box 5000
Iola, WI 54945
Phone: (715) 445-5000
Fax: (715)445-4053

How To Make & Repair
Leather Doll Bodies

By LaVonne Lutterman

Published By:
Jones Publishing, Incorporated
N7450 Aanstad Road
P.O. Box 5000
Iola, WI 54945
Phone: (715) 445-5000
Fax: (715) 445-4053

This book is available at special discounts for bulk purchases. For prices or other information contact Greg Bayer at the above address.

Third Printing
Printed in the United States

ISBN 1-879825-17-1

About the Author

LaVonne Lutterman is one of America's leading doll restorers. She began her career at the age of 13 when she sold her first oil portrait. After graduating from the Humboldt Institute in Minneapolis, Lutterman continued her artistic endeavors in Chicago and Sioux Falls, South Dakota.

It was back in Minnesota in 1960 that LaVonne began restoring dolls. Her focus at the time was porcelain, china and glass. In 1962 she began restoring antique dolls, and by 1964 she was making dolls. Soon after that, she was teaching dollmaking and restoration. LaVonne continues to teach at her studio in Minnesota and across the country at various workshops.

LaVonne is also the founder of the International Doll Restoration Artists Association (IDRAA). She created this association in 1986 when it became apparent that the need for doll repair and restoration was much larger than the number of qualified people available. IDRAA has established a code of ethics, and strives to educate and improve the quality of repair/restoration work. Currently, the IDRAA has over 500 members.

LaVonne's previously published books include *Make, Repair and Restore Eyes* and *Complete Composition*. This is the third printing of *How To Make & Repair Leather Doll Bodies*.

Outside of her life with repairing, restoring, and making dolls, LaVonne is married, has two children and three grandchildren.

Please Read This!

This book was produced for the entertainment and enlightenment of dollmakers. While every effort has been made to ensure that the information contained herein is correct and up-to-date, the editor, author, and publisher extend no warranty as to the accuracy or completeness of the information—there may be mistakes, both typographical and in content. Therefore, this text should be used only as a general guide and not as the ultimate source of information.

This book is sold with the understanding that the publisher is not engaged in rendering product endorsements or providing instruction as a substitute for appropriate training by qualified sources. Therefore, Jones Publishing, Inc. and the author, LaVonne Lutterman, shall have neither liability nor responsibility to any person or entity with respect to any loss or damage caused, or alleged to be caused, directly or indirectly, by the information contained in this book.

We hope that you enjoy reading *How To Make & Repair Leather Doll Bodies*.

Table of Contents

Repair
&
Restoration

Introduction

This text is intended to enable the reader to make and repair leather doll bodies. Beginning with a list of supplies and equipment, this book goes on to describe in detail what you need to know to make your own repairs: selecting leather, stretching it, marking patterns, and using sewing machines effectively on leather. Information is also added on attendant matters: how to stuff, clean, condition and dye the leather bodies. The descriptions are clear and simple to follow. We hope that you derive much enjoyment from the dolls whose lives will be extended by what you learn from the following pages.

Supplies & Equipment

Adhesives: see *glue*.

Aluminum Foil: Used for copying doll forms to recreate a pattern.

Awl: A sharp pointed instrument with a heavy wooden handle, used to pierce holes in leather.

Ball Point Pen: For marking flaws and patterns on the back (rough) side of the leather. Use a pen with permanent ink and test it to make certain it does not bleed through the leather.

Beeswax: Used to coat thread before sewing leather. It gives the thread added strength and prevents tangles.

Bull Dog: A type of fastener used to hold pieces of glued leather together.

Cabretta: A fine leather made from sheepskin. A cost-effective alternative to kidskin.

Cutting Tools: A single-edge razor blade and a sharp dressmaker's shears are essential

Dowel: A wooden rod, usually with a small diameter which can be used to stuff the doll body.

French Chalk: A talc for marking lines on fabrics.

Fun Fuse®: A thin, heat-fusible, web-like material used to bond two pieces together. Stitch Witchery® is an alternative product.

Glue: Choose a good quality white glue that remains flexible after drying, such as Sobo® or Leather Weld®.

Interfacing: A low heat iron-on adhesive fabric.

Needles — Glover's: Use these three-cornered needles when hand sewing leather. They are usually available in fabric shops and come in an assortment of sizes. The finer the needle, the lighter the weight of the skin it is intended to be used with.

Needles — Sewing Machine: Wedge-shaped leather needles for your sewing machine are available in assortment packs at fabric shops. Select size 11 needles when sewing lighter weight leather such as kidskin and cape skin (cabretta), or size 14 when sewing firm cape skin. Choose size 16 for heavy leather.

Paper — Brown Bag: When pressing leather, use a heavy brown paper bag as a substitute for a press cloth.

Paper — Index Card: Use index cards or paper of similar weight to transfer pattern pieces.

Paper Clips: Available in a variety of styles and sizes. Use them instead of pins to hold pieces of glued leather together.

Pattern Hold: Available in an aerosol can. Use this to keep pieces in place while cutting and marking. When applied to the wrong side of a pattern, it makes the pieces pressure sensitive.

Plywood: Select a 1/2 or 3/8 inch thick piece on which to stretch and dry leather.

Press Cloth: Use a dry press cloth on the wrong (back) side of the leather when pressing.

Presser Foot: Always use a straight stitch presser foot on your machine when sewing leather. A roller presser foot is excellent to use for top stitching. A Teflon® coated foot is available for some machines and is extremely helpful when working with thick, heavy leather.

Shears — Pinking: Gives cut edges a finished look and eliminates the need to hand sew the edges around the neck line and arms.

Shears — Scalloping: Scalloping shears add a truly professional, finished look to cut edges and eliminates the need to hand finish them. Scalloping shears are available through fabric stores and sewing centers.

Skiving Knife: A knife designed to cut leather. The brand X-Acto® is the most common accepted alternative to a skiving knife.

Stitch Witchery®: A thin, heat-fusible, web-like material used to bond two pieces together. An alternative product is Fun Fuse®.

Tape — Mending: Can be ironed on the wrong side of the leather to reinforce weak areas.

Tape — Transparent: Used to hold pattern pieces in place while cutting the leather.

Thread: Use a mercerized cotton thread such as Coats and Clarks® Dual Duty Plus.

Thumbtacks: Used as fasteners for stretching the leather.

Wooden Mallet: Used to flatten seams, the mallet's head should be covered with a piece of leather (held in place with glue or a rubber band).

Type of Leather Used for Doll Bodies

Most antique leather doll bodies were made from kidskin, a soft and pliable, yet exceptionally sturdy, goatskin. Unfortunately, even when kidskin can be found on today's market, the price is prohibitive. Therefore, if you intend to restore or reproduce an antique leather body, you must find an appropriate substitute.

Cabretta, a readily available garment leather, has become the popular alternative for making and repairing doll bodies. Strong and smooth, it makes a good substitute for kidskin, especially when the skin is properly stretched.

Selecting Leather

Leather, such as cabretta, from small animals is usually sold by the skin. Because leather is not manufactured as fabric, there are many variations and flaws in the skins. The absence of set standards for grading leather demands that you learn to judge leather by sight and feel. Therefore, you should closely inspect several skins before making a purchase.

When you purchase cabretta, the size of the animal will determine the size of the skin. The skin is run through a computer which measures the overall area of each skin, and it is priced accordingly (by the square foot). Most cabretta skins range in size from 6 to 8 square feet.

Locating the Grain in Leather

Leather has a distinct grain. However, unlike the grain in fabric, the grain in leather does not run straight across or straight down the skin. It may extend a short distance and then veer off in another direction. The basic grain in leather runs along the backbone of the animal hide (see illustration #1) and the pattern is usually cut with the grain of the leather. Keep in mind that leather does stretch. The crosswise grain has more stretch than the length-wise grain.

Illustration #1

REAR   GRAIN   FRONT

To locate the grain in leather, first place the skin on a soft, clean padded surface which will prevent scuffing and soiling as you work. With the rough (wrong) side of the hide facing you, grip a small section of the leather with your thumb and forefingers (see illustration #2). Pull the

Illustration #2

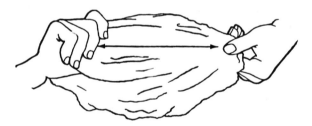

section of leather just as you would pull fabric if you were trying to find the bias. Work only one area (6-8 inches) at a time. Rotate the leather as you work around the area. Mark the direction of the grain on the back of the leather. Repeat until you have grained and marked the entire skin.

Stretching the Leather

Never stretch leather without first locating and marking the grain. The biggest drawback about working with cabretta is its incredible amount of stretch. This can be a problem or an advantage, depending on how the leather is prepared. When a skin is properly grained and stretched, it produces a much larger skin.

Begin by spraying the back (rough) side of the leather with a fine mist of lukewarm water. An old household cleaner bottle works well (make certain it has been thoroughly washed and rinsed). Mist the skin slightly, then wait 10 minutes.

Soak a bath towel in warm water. Wring it out until it is as dry as possible. Place the damp towel on the back (rough) side of the skin, entirely covering the surface of the leather with it. Roll the towel and skin up together and place them in a tightly closed plastic bag until the moisture equalizes. It usually takes one to two hours.

Remove the leather from the bag. Begin to gently pull and stretch the leather. If you have someone helping you, ask your helper to grasp the opposite side of the skin and hold it while you pull. Pull gently until you have stretched the leather in that particular area. Then, move to a new section and repeat the process until you have made a full circle around the skin. Repeat several times until you have pulled the skin from all directions. If you must work alone, grasp the leather in the center of the skin and hold it with one hand while you pull around the edges of the skin with the other hand.

After you have completed this primary stretching, fasten the skin down to a piece of 1/2 or 3/8th inch plywood. Place the leather on the board with the smooth (right) side facing you so it is not damaged by tiny splinters of wood. Proceed by fastening the skin to the board by placing thumb tacks or staples along the outer edge of the skin, working in the following manner.

Tack the center of one edge of the skin to the plywood, then pull and stretch the skin that is directly opposite it until the leather is as taut as possible, and fasten this edge to the board. Work a small area at a time, from one center edge to the opposite center edge. For example, if you fasten the north edge of the skin first, you must stretch and fasten the south (opposite) side next. Proceed to fasten the east edge of the skin, then stretch the west edge and fasten it next (see illustration #3).

After fastening the four center edges, repeat the stretching process. Pull and stretch the skin on both sides of one of the tacked areas and tack it down. Move to the opposite side of the board; stretch and fasten the leather on both sides of the original tack or staple. Repeat the process, working from the center to the outside edges until the leather is completely stretched and fastened to the board. When you reach a corner, stretch the skin against the opposite corner.

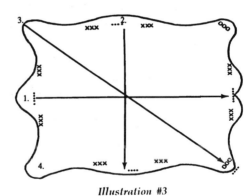

Illustration #3

After the leather is on the board for about one hour, inspect it. Loosen the staples or tacks along one edge of the leather to see if there is any additional stretch. If so, tighten any areas that have slack, and refasten the edges. Keep in mind that a hide's greatest strength is across the center of the back, from the neck to the rump. Use extra care when retightening the leather, especially where flaws or natural weak spots exist.

After restretching the skin, put the board up against a wall, where it will be out of the way, and let the leather dry naturally. The drying time depends on the temperature and humidity in the room and the amount of moisture in the hide. Drying can vary from a day or two to a week depending on these factors. If you are in a hurry, increase the temperature in the room slightly and/or place the leather in front of a fan. Never try to rush the drying process by exposing the leather to extreme heat. Excessive heat will make the leather brittle.

Marking the Pattern on the Leather

Begin by tracing the pattern onto a piece of tissue paper, and make any necessasry adjustments on the tissue paper in order to preserve your original pattern. Dolls vary greatly in size. Measure the shoulderplate and any bisque or china parts that must fit the leather body. If necessary, re-draw the correct lines on the tissue paper. After adjusting the pattern on tissue paper, transfer it to a piece of lightweight cardboard or an index card.

Place the leather on a clean, smooth surface with the rough (wrong) side up. Traditional methods of marking cannot be used when working with leather. Use 3M® Magic Transparent Tape to hold the pattern in position where you would otherwise pin it. Or, spray the pieces with Pattern Hold® to keep them in place while you trace them on the leather. As you lay out the pattern, match the grain lines on the pattern to the grain of the skin. Avoid using any areas that contain weak or damaged leather unless they have been reinforced with iron-on tape.

Reverse the pattern pieces when applicable. Never cut folded leather. If the pattern states "place on fold," draw one half of the pattern on the skin, then reverse the pattern. Check to make certain the reversed piece is correctly aligned, then draw around it to make one complete piece. After you tape the pattern pieces to the skin, draw around them precisely to ensure accuracy. Work with a light touch to prevent damaging the leather.

Make certain that pairs, such as arms and leg parts, are cut from a piece of leather that has the same thickness and texture. These pieces must be identical. After all, you want them to match when the body is finished.

Consider the thickness and texture of the leather as you lay out the pattern. A doll's torso is the largest area and should be made from the strongest leather. Select a piece of leather from the back or neck, where the hide is tough. Gussets and the oval pieces of leather, which go into the leg of a pin jointed (universal) style body, are not usually visible when the body is completed. Cut these pieces from thin leather that have a heavy grain and coarse texture.

After tracing the pattern onto the leather, cut the leather into sections before you cut out the individual pieces. Sections are easier to handle and there is less chance of miscutting or pulling the leather out of shape while you work. Use an exceptionally sharp scissors and a smooth cutting motion. Do not "chop" at the leather as you cut or you will produce a jagged edge. Operate the blades of the scissors with one hand and guide the leather through them with the other.

Inspect the cut pieces to make sure they are cut on the grain. Check for cutting accuracy, too. To test a piece, fold it in the center and match the corners. If a piece is cut on the grain, when it is folded and held up, the side seams should match and not create folds in the leather. The piece should lie flat. When a piece is not cut on the grain, it is best to recut it. If it is only slightly off in length, it can be trimmed — provided the difference is minute and does not significantly alter the length of the part. Remember, any corresponding part must also be trimmed accordingly.

As you assemble the pieces, the warmth and moisture from your hands may soften the leather and make it remarkably stretchable. However, when it dries, it will again become firm.

Lining the Doll Body

Bodies over 20 inches long should be completely lined to prevent excess stretching while sewing and stuffing the body. Following the body pattern, cut the lining from a piece of muslin. Glue the lining to the back (rough) side of the corresponding leather piece using the following method: mix equal parts of water and a clear-drying flexible glue such as Sobo® or Leather Weld®. Do not use rubber cement and do not saturate the leather. Apply the glue to the leather's surface, stopping 1/8th of an inch from the edge of the seam allowance. Do not apply the glue any closer to the seam allowance in order to avoid sewing through the adhesive when you assemble the body. Let the pieces dry completely before you assemble the body.

Finally, press the muslin lining onto the leather. An alternate method of lining the body is to bond a liner to the body with a web bonding material or an iron-on facing material. If you use brand name webbing such as Fun Fuse® or Stitch Witchery®, sandwich the fusing material between the leather and the fabric liner. Press into place with a warm iron placed on the fabric. Examine the piece and adjust the alignment as required.

Adjusting the Shoulder Area

Most antique dolls, even those with the same size and style of body, vary greatly in the size and shape of the shoulderplate. Therefore, make any adjustments on a copy of the original pattern. You should have already traced a copy onto tissue paper.

Copy the shoulderplate of the doll using a piece of aluminum foil. Press the foil against the shoulderplate and trace around it to make the pattern. To mark the centerfront on the pattern, slash the pattern on the centerfront line, then cut out the neck opening (see illustration #4A).

Place the foil pattern on the doll, over the shoulderplate. Mark the shoulder seams (mold lines) on the foil. Remove the pattern from the doll and fold it in half. Align the marks for the shoulder seams and the centerfront. Mark the centerback. Fold the pattern in the opposite direction. Line up the centerfront and centerback. Check the marks at the shoulders. Correct and adjust as necessary.

Trace the commercial pattern onto a piece of tissue paper. Compare the commercial pattern to your adjusted foil pattern. Place the neck edges together and match the centerfronts. Trace the new shoulder area from the adjusted (foil) pattern onto the

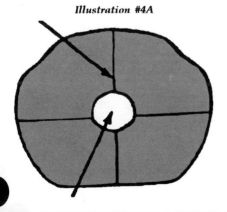

Illustration #4A

tissue paper pattern. Draw a new 1/4 inch wide seam allowance on the adjusted tissue paper pattern. This allowance is drawn just above (to the outside edge) of the adjusted pattern. Continue the 1/4 inch seam allowance until you reach the shoulder seam line, then increase it to 3/4 inch. This allows a little extra for lapping the front shoulder tabs over the back.

Mark the centerfront and the shoulders. Do not change the pattern in the area that lies half way between the neck line and the underarm.

Repeat the process to mark the remaining half (either front or back) of the pattern.

Make a new pattern by combining the front of the commercial pattern with the front of your adjusted pattern. Match the newly drawn seam allowance to the commercial pattern. Repeat for the back of the pattern. Fit the new pattern to the doll's shoulderplate and adjust as needed (see illustration #4B). If the torso adjustment is significant, adjust the torso liner accordingly. After adjusting the pattern, transfer it to lightweight cardboard or index cards.

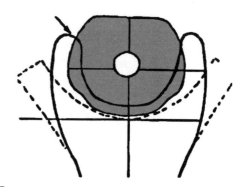

Illustration #4B

Thread

Basting stitches are a temporary means of holding two pieces of material together until they can be machine sewn. Any kind of good quality thread can be used for basting. For most sewing, either by hand or machine, a cotton wrapped polyester thread is preferred. Ordinary cotton thread alone is not recommended because of its poor durability. Nylon thread can be used although it produces a high amount of static electricity which can make sewing difficult. If you prefer nylon thread, attach a strip of grounding copper to the sewing machine so it presses against the spool of thread. When machine sewing leather, I strongly suggest using either Coats and Clarks® Dual Duty Plus or a taslon nylon thread.

Before you begin hand sewing, run your thread over some beeswax to coat it. This process strengthens the thread, eliminates those annoying tangles, and allows the thread to slip easily through the leather.

Basting

Basting is an extremely important step when sewing leather, so never try to eliminate it. If you do try to eliminate basting, the leather will slip, drag, and pull out of shape as it feeds through the machine, resulting in a distorted body.

To baste leather by hand, use a glover's needle with a three-cornered blade point to penetrate the leather. Use a size 5 or 6 needle for basting lightweight leather such as kidskin and cabretta. Glover's needles are available at fabric and sewing centers in packs of assorted sizes.

Use a modified form of the running stitch instead of an overcast stitch when you baste leather. The leather will slip out of alignment if you overcast your stitches. Keep the stitches small and work as near the edge of the leather as possible so the basting re-

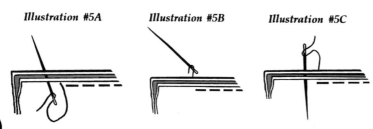

Illustration #5A   *Illustration #5B*   *Illustration #5C*

mains outside the seam allowance. No basting stitches should be visible after machine sewing the leather. Align the two pieces of leather and hold them together tightly. Push the needle down into the leather and pull it out through the opposite end (see illustrations #5A-C). Repeat. Although each stitch is made individually, the result will look like a running stitch which is made by making several small stitches at a time before pulling the thread through.

Basting With Glue or Cement

You can save time and effort by basting the leather with rubber cement or a flexible white glue. The glue or cement you use must remain flexible, such as Sobo® or Leather Weld® brand glues. When a piece of leather must be eased into place, as is often the case with leather bodies, basting with glue offers a distinct advantage because glue contains moisture that softens the leather and makes it stretch.

Although these adhesives remain flexible, you must be careful not to apply them past the seam line. Apply the adhesive halfway between the edge of the leather and the seam line (see illustration #6A). Do not let it extend beyond that point. If you sew into a carelessly applied adhesive, it will make the needle tacky and will eventually gum up the machine. Apply the adhesive with a brush, tooth pick, ear syringe, or soft plastic bottle with a tiny applicator tip. If you use an applicator bottle, make certain the tip is small so you have full control over the amount of adhesive it releases.

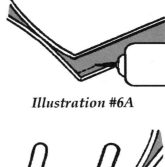

Illustration #6A

Illustration #6B

To begin, first apply the glue to the edge of the piece of leather that must be stretched and eased. Let the piece lay for a few moments while the leather absorbs some of the moisture. Add a little more adhesive to the piece and apply a tiny line of glue to the remaining piece. The first piece, which is saturated with glue, will conform easily to the second piece. Apply the adhesive carefully to both of the pieces of leather to avoid getting adhesive on the seam line.

If you accidentally apply adhesive to the inside of the seam line, immediately wipe it away with a damp cloth. When working with rubber cement, make a little "glue ball" and let it dry. Use it like an eraser to remove any excess cement.

After the two pieces of leather are joined with an adhesive, press them between your fingers and hold them together with a bull dog fastener or paper clips until they dry (see illustration #6B). Never pin leather. Pins weaken the leather and make puncture marks that cannot be removed.

The Sewing Machine

Once the machine is properly adjusted, machine sewing leather is no more difficult than sewing fabric. Newer machines often have these adjustments calibrated. If you have an older machine, experiment with a few scraps of leather to find the best setting.

Before you make any adjustments, inspect the machine. It should be clean and well oiled. Wipe up any excess oil and brush away any loose threads and particles of lint. Check to make certain the bobbin is running freely and there are no tiny particles of thread caught in the mechanism or bobbin case.

Attach a straight-stitch presser foot, then adjust it. Although leather is thicker than cloth, it is spongy so you can use less pressure. To check the presser foot, stitch on a few scraps of leather. If sewing a lined body, use pieces of the lined leather to test and adjust the machine. If necessary, lighten the pressure a little to accommodate the extra thickness of the leather. If you have a problem adjusting the machine, envelop the leather in a piece of tissue paper to help it slide through the machine. You may prefer using a dual feed, even feed, Teflon® coated, or roller foot. If your machine is a "dial a stitch," make certain that it is set for straight stitching. If it has a "swing" needle, position the needle as far to the right as possible.

Generally, set the machine to between 7 and 10 stitches per inch and test the length of the stitch on a scrap of leather. Since, leather is thicker than cloth, you should use a slightly longer stitch. If the stitch is too small, it will shred the leather and weaken the seams. If the leather is exceptionally soft and thin, increase the stitches to as many as 12 per inch, or reduce it to 8 for exceptionally thick leather. When topstitching, increase the length of the stitch to improve the appearance of the stitching.

Use a leather needle in your machine. The blade point easily penetrates a layer of leather. Keep in mind that the smaller the needle, the neater the stitch. Use a size 11 needle, which is intended for lightweight suede and capeskin (cabretta).

Concern yourself only with adjusting the top thread tension The lower (bobbin) tension is usually set at the factory and does not need to be changed. Test the machine on a folded piece of scrap leather or leather with a lining. If the tension is too loose, the thread will form balls or loops along the bottom of the seam (see illustration #7A). Increase the tension by turning the tension knob to a higher number. If the thread cuts into the leather, loops on the top side of the seam, or breaks, reduce the tension because it is too tight. When the stitches on both sides of the leather look alike, the machine is in adjustment (see illustration #7B). Once the tension is adjusted, there is no need to change it or make further adjustment while sewing the body.

Illustration #7A: No Adjustment Required

Illustration #7B: Upper (White) Thread is Too Loose

Tips for Sewing Leather With a Machine

Ease the pieces into the machine and carefully guide them to prevent stretching the leather. Round the corners to eliminate bulk whenever possible. When attaching a cloth lining to leather, place the cloth on top of the leather and stitch into the fabric.

All darts should be opened after sewing. Place a little glue along the edge of the surplus leather, then press or pound the dart so it lays and stays flat.

When two seams intersect, press the joint with a warm iron. Use a brown paper bag or press cloth while you work. Never use steam. Glue the excess seam allowance, at the joint, then pound it flat. After the glue dries, lift the corners of the seam allowance and trim it to remove any bulk. The seam will lay flat with far less tension on it.

If you have a roller or Teflon® coated presser foot, use it when top-stitching. If not, place a piece of tissue paper under the pressure foot. This gives you better control so your stitching is more accurate.

The bulk of the leather can be removed from a curved seam by cutting small triangular shaped wedges from the seam allowance after the seam is machine sewn. If the item is small, the excess leather in the seam allowance can be slashed with a sharp razor blade rather than cutting out triangles. Either way, be careful not to cut into the stitching (seam) line. If the excess seam allowance is open and glued flat, remove the pieces before cementing the seams.

Illustration #8

To make easing the pieces of leather effortless, snip the leather at intervals (see illustration #8) before sewing the seam. After closing the seam, clip the notches to help retain the curve. Finish both ends of the seam by tying the loose ends of the threads in a knot rather than backstitching. Backstitching causes punctures marks from the needle that cannot be removed, so work slowly and carefully.

Snip The Leather At This Point Before Sewing The Seam

After Sewing The Seam, Clip the Notches (indicated by the shaded area).

After sewing leather, sprinkle it with a little talc to ease the process of turning it right side out.

Stuffing Bodies

The appearance of a doll body, whether cloth or leather, depends not only on your skill and exactness during the process of making it, but also on your ability to stuff it properly. Stuffing a doll body requires time, practice, and patience. There is more to it than just jamming the body full of stuffing. Improper packing will produce strange wrinkles, lumps, and limp, misshapen bodies.

An assortment of items found around the house can generally serve as tools needed for stuffing leather bodies: the handles of wooden spoons, crochet hooks, and ball point pens (be sure they have the cap over the end to prevent piercing the body material). Just about anything with a round end can be used. Some of the best stuffing tools are dowels in various diameters with the ends filed and sanded so that they are smooth and round. Use dowels with small diameters to reach into feet and hands, and ones with larger diameters for torsos. While cloth dolls are meant to be soft and cuddly, leather bodies must be able to support bisque heads. Fill the leather body with enough stuffing to make it extra firm without causing a deformity. Leather which is tightly packed to make a rigid body will not return to its original shape after it is stretched.

Leather bodies are usually stuffed with either ground cork or sifted sawdust. Cork is lightweight and nice to work with. The body can be packed tightly and still remain fairly lightweight. Cork, which is considerably more expensive than sawdust, is sometimes available through doll supply companies. The most dependable, reasonably priced supplier of granulated cork that I know of is a taxidermy supply company. Write to Van Dyke's, P.O. Box 278, Woonsocket, SD 57385 or call (605)796-4425, and ask for their taxidermy catalog. Their catalog also offers excelsior, paper pulp, paint, and various other materials used in doll rebuilding.

If you use sawdust to fill leather bodies, you may either purchase it presifted from a doll supply company, or sift it yourself. Sawdust must be completely dry before you use it to pack a doll body. Otherwise it will shrink as it dries, eventually producing a limp, sagging doll body. No special equipment is required to sift the sawdust. A large kitchen strainer is quite satisfactory. The mesh is small enough to ensure that the sawdust will be smooth and free of lumps that could cause the body to be bumpy. If using large quantities of sawdust on a regular basis, you may prefer using a larger sifter.

You can make a sifter yourself by stapling a piece of ordinary window screen to a wooden frame made from 1" x 2" lumber. Arrange the 1 x 2s so the side of the box is 2 inches high to help contain the sawdust and reduce spillage. Another way to construct a sifter is to cut a ring, 4 inches wide, from the top of an old plastic pail. Use a heavy-duty stapler to fasten a piece of nylon screen to the rim. Eureka! You have a sifter that will fit over the rim of an identical pail. If a heavy-duty stapler isn't available, punch holes in the upper rim of the plastic with an awl or ice pick. Space the holes about 1 inch apart, use wire to "sew" the screen to the plastic rim.

When restuffing a repaired doll body, reuse the original stuffing. It is an important part of the doll. If some stuffing was lost through the years, finish filling the body with a material that closely resembles the original . Note: If you restuff a limp old leather body, give it a bit more strength by working a short wooden dowel down inside the body. Pack stuffing tightly around the stick to keep the body from bending at the waist.

Stuffing a body is an art. You must constantly stop and appraise your work. You must mold and sculpt the shape of the body as you fill it. Areas with darts or a rounded contour must be shaped and formed with one hand while you use the other to fill and pack the stuffing.

When you stuff a leather body, fold the torso down about 3/4ths of the way before you begin (see illustration #9). This helps keep sawdust from creeping between the muslin liner and the leather. When cork or sawdust accumulates between the body and the liner, ugly little bumps form on the body unless they are removed, which is no easy task. Folding the torso down helps to eliminate this problem.

Illustration #9

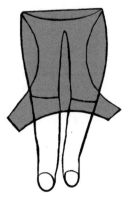

When you stuff a leather body, add the stuffing in small amounts. Pack and shape the first bit of stuffing before you add more. Spoon the stuffing into each leg until it is about 1/3rd full, then pack the sawdust into the legs. Alternate legs as you work. At each filling, consider the relationship between the size of the body and the amount of stuffing you are adding to the body. Add gradually and pack the stuffing into place before adding more. Stop frequently to compare the size and shape of the legs. When you evaluate your work, ask yourself, "Is one arm or leg slightly larger than the other?" If you grained and stretched the leather, followed your pattern, aligned, trimmed, and kept the seams evenly spaced, then you didn't goof when you made the body — you just stuffed one limb a bit more than the other. Uniformity doesn't just happen. You must work at it. Constantly check the pieces and compare the stuffed limb to the one you are filling. Do this frequently so you can make the corrections immediately—while you can still reach the area easily. When the limbs are firmly packed and the proportions are identical, add more stuffing.

Continue packing and comparing until you reach the knee gusset. Check to see that both legs are packed as tightly as possible, then begin to fill the lower portion of the knee gusset (see illustration #10). Push the seam open, then press and pack sawdust into the lower half of the knee gusset. Use your thumb to apply pressure to the gusset from the outside of the body. Pack the sawdust into place until the lower edge of the gusset is firm and lies perfectly flat.

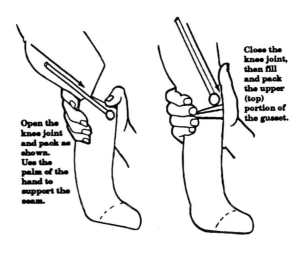

Illustration #10

Hold the leg in your hand so the knee gusset is closed and the leg is fully extended. Add more stuffing and pack the upper half of the knee gusset. If you turned the torso down before you began filling the body, you can reach in and pack the stuffing with your thumb. Use the eraser end of a pencil to tamp it as you work. Continue packing the body until you reach the hip gusset. The hip gusset is filled and packed by using the same method you used for the knee gusset. Keep alternating sides of the body as you work, and check your work frequently.

After the body is stuffed to the top of the hip line, roll the torso up a little and begin filling the it. Roll, fill, and pack until you reach the top of the body. Work slowly and carefully. Do not push directly against the edge of the leather with your tools. Too much direct force against the leather can stretch it and cause a bulge that is difficult, if not impossible, to remove. Support the seams with the palm of your hand as you work. This prevents you from pushing so hard that you break the stitches and split the seam.

As you reach the top of the body, begin to fit the shoulderplate. When the body is firm and the shoulderplate fits snugly, cover the sawdust with a thin layer of cotton batting or poly-fil® and then close the liner.

When stuffing the arms on leather bodies, do not pack them as firmly as the body itself. The arms only have to be firm enough to hold their shape. The upper part of the arm, where it fastens into the body, should be stuffed with a little cotton. Then press it firmly between your fingers to flatten it a little. Upper arms must be relatively flat if they are going to hang nicely.

Cleaning Old Kidskin Leather Bodies

There are several methods of cleaning old kidskin leather bodies. The one you choose should be determined by the degree of soil on the leather body.

Before you begin, it is important to realize that old doll bodies made of kidskin were dyed. During the process of cleaning the body, a certain amount of dye is removed and the natural color of the leather is sometimes exposed. The amount of dye removed by cleaning depends largely on the degree of soil and the type of cleaner you use. After the body is cleaned, and conditioned if necessary, the dye will be renewed. Dry, brittle, and cracked leather must be conditioned to make it soft and supple. It should be cleaned before it is conditioned; failure to do so forces the soil deep into the leather.

Lightly soiled leather can usually be cleaned without moisture. Rub the leather with a dry, absorbent substance such as powdered alum, cream of tartar, Fuller's Earth®, bread crumbs, or corn meal. Gently rub the body with the cleaning material and wipe it off with a soft flannel cloth. Replace the cleaning powder when it becomes soiled and rotate your cloth to a clean area as you wipe the leather to pick up loose soil.

Stained leather should be treated to remove as much of the stain as possible before cleaning. Otherwise the stain can seep through and discolor the new finish. Treat greasy stains by placing several layers of folded facial tissue over the stain. Press with a warm iron. Repeat as often as needed and keep rotating the facial tissue to a clean area as it absorbs the grease. Remove large oil and grease stains by applying egg white to them. Then, place the leather in the sun for several hours until it is dry. Wipe the leather with a soft cloth. Or, you may cover greasy stains with a paste made from a combination of Fuller's Earth® and water. Let the leather stand until it is dry, wipe the paste off with a soft flannel cloth. Repeat the process as necessary. Small oil and grease stains may be removed by wiping the area with a soft cloth dipped in alcohol.

Treat mildew after you clean the leather. Although the treatment may not completely remove mildew, it does control the growth and prevents it from bleeding through onto the new dye. Apply a little petroleum jelly to the affected areas and then wipe it off with a clean, soft cloth. Repeat the process until as much of the stain is removed as possible. Dust with powdered alum to absorb any of the excess petroleum jelly. Wipe off the powder with a soft cloth. Repeat several times. Finish by gently wiping each spot with a cloth that has been dampened with vinegar.

Always test an ink stain with a little water to see if the ink runs. If it does, it is probably an ink composed of cosin, nigrosine, or some other type of coal tar base. Removing such ink stains is imperative, for they are certain to bleed into the new dye. To clean these types of ink, make a thick paste of water and baking soda. Apply it to the stain and rub it a little, working from the outer edge toward the center. As the paste absorbs the ink, wipe it off, and apply more paste. Keep the paste moist while you work and remove as much of the stain as you possibly can. Be careful not to saturate the leather.

Ink stains that do not run can be remarkably difficult to cover with dye, so they should be completely removed whenever possible, or at least treated and lightened. Get a little oxalic acid from the drugstore. Mix it with water and apply it to the leather in the form of a thin paste. When the paste absorbs as much of the ink as it is going to, wipe the area with household ammonia and water to neutralize the acid.

Ammonia and a mild white bar soap make an inexpensive, effective leather cleaner for bodies with moderate to heavy soil. Dip a clean white flannel cloth in a little household ammonia, then lightly rub it over a bar of white soap. Gently wipe the soiled body with this cloth, working a small area at a time. Lift the dirt from the surface; do not rub it in. You must repeat this process several times before an area will come clean. Do not saturate the leather. If the area in which you are working becomes damp, stop and let it dry. If the body is heavily soiled, clean it, let it dry, and then repeat the entire cleaning process. Change the cloth as it begins to pick up soil.

There are many commercial leather cleaner/conditioner combinations on the market. However, cleaning and conditioning are usually better done in two separate steps. Although the products are safe and effective when used on new leather, they should not be used on exceptionally old, dry, or brittle leather. Keep in mind that whenever you work with a cleaner/conditioner, a large amount of the dirt and grime is driven deep into the leather. Yet, the object of cleaning is to lift and remove the soil. Old, dry leather absorbs cleaner/conditioner so quickly that it is impossible to wipe away the soil before it is absorbed. Most cleaner/conditioners soften the leather too much, too quickly. The old leather may become soft and mushy; it cannot be wiped without pilling (rubbing off into tiny balls).

When the body is clean, let it air dry for a full day before you condition it. The leather must dry thoroughly between each step—cleaning, conditioning, and dyeing.

Conditioning Leather

After the leather is clean and dry, condition it. Leather that is soft and supple does not require deep conditioning. Wipe a thin coating of conditioner on the body and let it stand until the conditioner is absorbed and the leather is dry.

When properly done, conditioning is usually a slow process. Old, dry, and brittle leather must be treated gently. It is fragile and easily damaged by careless handling.

Castor oil or Neet's-Foot® oil are both excellent for conditioning leather. If you choose Neet's-Foot® oil, make certain you purchase refined, not raw, oil. Although raw oil will condition the leather without damaging it, it has a dark color which will discolor leather more than the refined oil. Refined Neet's-Foot® oil is available at drug stores, leather goods stores, and saddle shops. Both castor and Neet's-Foot® oil are expensive, but they are highly effective — and a little goes a long way. If necessary, apply the conditioner repeatedly over a period of several days. Each time the body is conditioned, the leather becomes more pliable and easier to work with.

To condition extremely dry and fragile bodies, heat the oil. Leather absorbs warm oil much more quickly. Warm it just to the point where it is still comfortable to the touch. Carefully apply the warm oil with a silk sponge. Work gently, lightly smoothing the oil over the surface. Do not attempt to rub it into the leather.

Some areas of the leather will absorb the oil quickly and become dull looking while others will remain glossy. After the leather is oiled, wait an hour. Then reheat the oil and apply it *only* to the glossy patches. Let the doll stand overnight to absorb the oil before you apply more. Feel the leather before you apply the next coat of oil. If it is extremely dry and brittle, repeat the process.

After two light treatments, even the driest body begins to feel soft and pliable. If the leather requires additional conditioning at that point, heating the oil is unnecessary. Just wipe it on. Or, mix equal amounts of lanolin and Neet's Foot® oil for an extremely effective conditioner. Conditioning brittle leather is a slow job, but it is worth the effort. Work carefully, one step at a time. Let the leather dry between each thin application of conditioner.

To improve the appearance of scuffed, fuzzy looking leather, polish the leather with French chalk or a fine pumice. After the conditioner is completely dry, but before you dye the leather, gently wipe the pumice or chalk over the area with a soft cloth.

Pin holes in leather can be partially disguised by filling each tiny hole with a dot of flexible white glue. Apply a drop of glue to each hole using a toothpick or the end of a pin. After the glue dries, examine the hole. It should be filled and level with the surface of the leather. If not, apply another tiny drop of glue. When it dries, dye the leather to disguise the holes and make them almost invisible.

Dying the Leather Body

Leather should be cleaned, conditioned, and repaired before it is dyed. Cleaning and conditioning leather removes some of the dye, some areas may take on the yellow-tan color of natural leather. To correct this problem and conceal the natural color of the leather, it must be covered by an application of dye. However, not all leather needs to be dyed, so only dye it when absolutely necessary.

Leather dye is available from leather supply and shoe stores. If you go to a shoe store, make certain you get leather dye, not shoe polish; there is a difference. The two brand names that I use most frequently are Cova Dye® from Tandy Leather Co. and Magix® Shoe Color Spray.

Cova Dye® comes in a cream form and is slightly thicker than shoe polish. It is an acrylic-based dye that can be thinned with water to the consistency of paint or shoe polish. Apply several thin coats and let each one dry completely before adding another. I find that a soft poly sponge with a fine texture or a little poly paint pad produces excellent results when used to apply this type of dye. Dip the sponge or pad in the dye and apply a thin layer on and into the leather. After the first coat has dried, repeat the process, applying the dye in the opposite direction .

Magix® Shoe Color Spray comes in an aerosol can. Again, several thin coats are better than one thick one. To avoid difficulty in holding the doll while you work, suspend the body and then spray it. If you happen to have one of those huge old hat pins or a long needle, run it through the muslin liner at the top of the body. Attach a wire to each end of the pin or needle and suspend the body from the attached wires. If you prefer, you may run a wire through the torso liner, or sew or staple a fabric loop to the muslin liner, and suspend the body from it.

If the body has gussets, prop the gussets open, dye them, and let them dry for 24 hours before dying the rest of the body. If the points of contact are not completely dry, the parts will stick to each other and ruin the job. After the points of contact are thoroughly dry, dye the rest of the body.

Note: Tint the dye to simulate the color of the old leather. Mix colors into the white dye. If the dye is a water-based or acrylic dye, you can color it with bisque stain or dry china paint.

Pressing Leather

Leather is pressed by the heat and the weight of the iron. Use a moderately warm iron with a brown paper bag or a press cloth placed on top of the leather. Move the iron constantly to avoid overheating the leather. Do not use steam. As long as you use a press cloth or a piece of brown paper between the iron and the leather, cabretta and kidskin can both be pressed on either the right (finished) side or the wrong (rough) side of the leather.

To repair old leather with iron-on mending tape, Stitch Witchery® or Fun Fuse®, or iron-on interfacing, set the iron on a moderately low temperature. Do not move it back and forth, simply press down. Be careful to avoid overheating.

Repairing Leather Bodies

Leather bodies, even those in the most deplorable condition, can usually be salvaged. An old leather body with weak leather and torn seams may appear to be quite hopeless. But once you understand the basics of cleaning, repairing, and assembly, the work can be accomplished quite easily.

Before you begin making a repair, you need a working knowledge of how the old bodies were made and assembled. Study the patterns and assembly directions in this book. Use leather or fabric scraps to practice making a gusseted body and a pin jointed (universal) body. Once you make and assemble them, you will be secure in your knowledge and will hopefully never have a problem when it comes to knowing how to take apart and re-assemble an old body. Clean and condition the body before you begin the repair in order to prevent damaging brittle leather when you handle it. However, do not dye it until after you complete the repairs.

Routine problems when making repairs include weak seams, weak leather, and holes or splits in the leather. Damage around the little metal buttons that hold the limbs in place on pin-jointed (universal) bodies is common for that type of body. Torn leather and weak seams around gussets are also a routine problem with that body style.

Before you begin, cover your work area with clean paper. It keeps the body clean and catches any cork or sawdust that leaks out while you work. Do not use newspaper to cover the work area; the ink easily rubs off and stains the leather.

It is almost impossible to make an invisible repair on a leather body. Your goal is to make the repair as strong and as neat as you possibly can. To accomplish this, you should, wherever possible , make repairs from inside the body.

Most repairs require a leather patch. It should be cut so that it extends at least 1/4 of an inch around the edges of the tear or split (from the top, bottom, and both sides). Cut the patch so that it is round or oval, not square or rectangular. Sharply angled corners tend to catch and lift. Put the patch wrong side (rough side) up on your work area and trim its edge to reduce the bulk. Trim the patch by cutting and beveling the edge of the leather with a sharp scissors held at a 45 degree angle. The edge of the

leather may also be trimmed with an X-Acto®
brand knife or a beveled edge leather-skiving
knife (see illustration #11). After the bulk is
reduced, flatten the edge even more by pound-
ing the patch with a padded wooden mallet.
The thinner the edge of the patch is, the better it
holds and the less noticeable it is if you must
apply it on the outside of the body.

Illustration #11

Repairing a Split or Tear
(without any pieces of leather missing)

This type of repair can almost always be accomplished from the inside of the body
by working a patch through the tear or by removing some of the stuffing so you can
easily reach the damaged area. The type of repair will depend on the location of the
damage, the condition of the leather, and the extent of the damage.

When the leather is strong and in good condition, it is usually easiest to make the
repair by removing some of the stuffing from the body, especially if the damage lies in
the upper one-half of the body. Open the torso liner and remove the stuffing until it is
one inch below the damaged area. Place the stuffing in a plastic bag and save it for later.
Brush the inside of the leather with a soft brush to remove any stuffing that clings to
the leather around the area where you intend to apply the patch. If stubborn bits of
sawdust refuse to be brushed away, pat them with a little bit of masking tape to lift
them. Pat, don't press, otherwise the tape could stick to the leather. If you must remove
all of the stuffing from the body, carefully turn it inside out before you begin making
your repair. After you remove as much of the stuffing as necessary, pack a thin layer
of cotton batting or poly-fil® brand stuffing over the remaining sawdust to keep the
loose particles of stuffing out of your way and out of the glue while you work.

Cut the patch to the correct shape and size, and skive the edges. Apply a moderately
thick coat of flexible clear drying glue to the smooth side of the patch. Cover the entire
surface of the patch with glue. Apply a similar coat of glue to the inner edges of the
leather around the tear. Immediately place the smooth (glued) side of the patch inside
the body and position it so the edges extend 1/4th of an inch around the entire tear.
Check the patch. The edges of the torn leather should be butted up to each other and
all jagged edges must be aligned. When the pieces are correctly aligned, press them
firmly against the patch, and hold it for a few minutes until the glue adheres.

To keep the patch in place, until the adhesive is completely dry, place a heavy
weight over the patch. Whenever possible, place the weight on the inside of the body.
Use any heavy object that fits the area. When working in a small area, I find that fishing
sinkers placed in a plastic bag work quite well. If the patch is small and the area is
difficult to reach, as it would be it if were in an arm or lower leg, carefully add stuffing
to the limb as soon as the glue begins to set rather than trying to place a weight on the
patch. Although this method is a little messy, the pressure from the stuffing will

hold the patch firmly in place until the glue dries.

Touch up the repair on the outside of the body after it is refilled. If there is a slight gap in the edges of the leather, fill it with a little glue. Use a damp cloth to wipe up any excess. After the glue dries, if there is still a gap or depression, fill it again until the surface of the leather is smooth. Then, apply a thin line of glue on top of the mended tear. Dip your fingers in a bit of water or use a moist brush to feather the edges of the glue. The object is to cover the outside of the mend with a thin, smooth layer of glue that will level the surface and make the repair less visible after the body is dyed. When dyeing leather with a thin skin of glue over the surface, first apply a thin coat of dye to the glue. Let it dry and repeat once more before dying the entire body.

When a small tear needs repair in an area that is difficult to reach, or in a body that is extremely fragile, the risk and effort of removing the stuffing is seldom worthwhile. Cut the patch and skive the edges. Then slide it through the split or rip in the body and work the patch into position with a crochet hook. Use a small syringe or soft plastic bottle with a small, point tip to apply the glue. Place the top of the glue applicator inside the body, between the body and the patch. Completely cover the patch with a liberal application of glue. Align the edges of the tear and press the body into place against the patch. Hold the edges together until the glue is set.

When a body needs additional stuffing and you want to make the repair through the rip without opening the body, the body must be filled before the repair is made. Carefully work additional stuffing through the opening in the tear to refill the body. Sometimes a small funnel is useful. Pack the stuffing as tightly as possible without damaging the leather. When the body is firm and the shape is correct, work the patch through the opening, then position it, and glue it into place.

At times, you may have to use a combination of these methods. For example, when repairing a fragile body that has lost stuffing through a small tear located below the waist, perhaps you will decide that it is safer to make the repair first. Remove the head, add the stuffing to the upper torso, and carefully work it down to fill the repaired area. Perhaps the leather around the damaged area is worn and fragile. Apply an extra large patch so you repair the split and reinforce the surrounding leather at the same time.

Repairing Holes

In order to repair a hole, you make the same type of decisions as when repairing a rip or tear. The condition of the leather and the size and location of the hole must be taken into account. You must also decide if the body is going to be repaired by working through the opening or by removing all or part of the stuffing.

When the hole is in a large area, such as the torso, use leather for a patch. If the hole is small or in an area where flexibility is important, the patch should be made with iron-on interfacing. No matter what method you use, always trim the edges of the hole to smooth jagged edges.

For a hole to be repaired with a leather patch, apply it inside the body to cover the hole. The patch should extend at least 1/4th of an inch beyond the edges of the hole. Place the patch in the body, align it, and glue the patch in place. Wipe off any excess glue on the outside of the body.

For a patch made of iron-on-interfacing, cut the interfacing patch so that it extends 1/2 inch beyond all the edges of the hole. Place it inside the body with the shiny side of the interfacing against the leather, facing you. Press the edges to keep the patch in place. Set the iron on a low to moderate heat. Place a piece of a brown paper bag over the hole and hold the iron in place on the edge of the hole for a few seconds. Remember, the repair requires only heat and pressure so don't slide the iron back and forth. Just press it onto the spot until the adhesive on the interfacing softens and bonds the leather. Since the adhesive on the interfacing remains soft and slippery when it is hot, wait a moment to let the adhesive cool and harden before moving on to the next spot. Continue working your way around the edge of the hole until the interfacing is bonded.

Apply a second patch of leather to cover the first patch in order to bring the hole level with the body. The second patch must be the same thickness as the leather in the body. Sort through your scrap leather until you find a piece that meets this requirement. If the leather is too thick, dip it in a little water and let it soak for a minute. Press it between paper towels to remove any excess moisture and carefully work it with your fingers. Gently pull and stretch the leather until it is the correct thickness. Tack the piece of leather to a board and let it dry completely before using it.

The second patch should be the same size and shape as the hole. Place it on top of the hole and begin to trim and fit it until the edges of the patch butt up against the edges of the hole. Apply a moderately thick coating of adhesive to the back (rough) side of the leather patch. Do not rub it in; let it soak into the leather. Apply a moderate coat of adhesive to the patched area on the body. Position the scrap patch on the body and press it into place. Carefully align the edges of the patch to the edges of the hole. Push or stretch the patch until it is perfectly aligned. Use a damp cloth to carefully wipe away any excess adhesive from the joint. Let the patch dry for 24 hours.

Before you dye the body, touch up the patch and dye it repeatedly. Feather the edges of each application to blend them into the surrounding area. Let the area dry completely before dyeing the entire body.

Reinforcing Weak Leather

To reinforce weak leather, the condition of the leather will determine the method to use. When beginning the process, check to make sure the leather is soft and supple. If it is, removing the stuffing and turning the body inside out is usually the fastest and easiest way to reinforce the leather. For this process, use a webbed fusing material such as Fun Fuse® or Stitch Witchery®. When the body is extremely fragile, removing the stuffing and reversing the body can do more harm than good. In this instance, use an iron-on-interfacing to make the repair.

When the leather is soft and can be turned inside out, remember to brush off all traces of stuffing that cling to the rough inner surface of the leather. To work with fusible webbing, put the fusing material on the leather body. Use a ball point pen to trace the outline of the area that is going to be reinforced. These fusing materials are thin and webby; you can see through them just as you could if you were using a piece of tissue paper. Cut the fusing material, following the outline. Use the piece as a pattern for an identical piece cut from cotton or lightweight muslin.

With the body turned inside out, place the fusing material against the rough side (inside) of the leather body and adjust it to the correct position against the body. Place cotton or muslin fabric over the fusing material. Put a piece of tissue paper on the fabric. Fun Fuse® and Stitch Witchery® are the bonding agents. When heated, the webbed fusing material melts and bonds the two pieces together. Use extra webbing, just as you would use additional glue (see illustration #12).

Illustration #12

Press with a moderately warm iron, held in place for a few seconds until the fusing agent melts and bonds the leather to the fabric. Press down with the iron, do not move it back and forth. Let the area cool before moving the iron to a new position. Repeat until the entire patch is fused to the leather. Let it cool completely, then carefully turn the body right side out.

For a fragile doll body, begin by gently pressing against the stuffing with your fingertips to move it away from the damaged area. Pack the stuffing into another portion of the body until there is enough room to slide the iron-on-interfacing patch inside. Cut the patch to the correct size and shape. Slip it inside the body and adjust it to the correct position. Make certain that it is lying smooth and flat. Gradually work the filling back and pack it against the interfacing. Keep checking the interfacing to see that it remains in place. When the patched area is firm, close the opening. To do this, put a press cloth or piece of heavy brown paper against the body — over the interfacing. Press with a moderate iron, held in place for at least 10 seconds to allow the bonding agent to soften and adhere.

Repairing a Split Seam

Repairing a split seam is not complicated, but it can be time consuming. Although the stuffing may be removed from the body, if the body is still strong and the area in need of repair is large, this is seldom needed. Even when the body is strong, the area in need of repair is often so small that the labor involved in removing and restuffing the body cannot be justified. When a small split is located in the lower part of the leg, the repair should be made from the outside of the body.

Begin by shifting the stuffing away from the seam. Work a crochet hook through the seam and into the body. Press the stuffing down against the opposite side of the leg rather than towards the feet. Move enough of the stuffing so you to have a little room to work. Cut a tiny patch of white cotton fabric large enough to cover the area that is damaged plus 1/4 inch beyond it. Use a crochet hook to work the cotton patch into the leg and arrange it over the stuffing in the area where the seam is split. Insert the nozzle of your adhesive applicator in the open seam and squeeze it until you have a thick coat of glue covering the cotton patch inside the leg. Match the edges of the seam and pinch them between your thumb and index finger to keep them in place while you work.

Press and massage the back of the leg (opposite the patch) between your fingers and the palm of your hand to work the stuffing back into place against the glued patch. Continue until the stuffing is firmly in place against the patch and the leg. Continue to hold the seam shut for a few minutes until the adhesive is thoroughly set. The pressure of the stuffing against the cotton patch is enough to keep it tight against the leather.

When the adhesive is set, release the seam. The seam may spread open a little, but it is still sealed from the inside so stuffing cannot leak through. If the space is wide and unattractive, apply a few drops of glue to the seam and hold it together with your fingers until the glue sets.

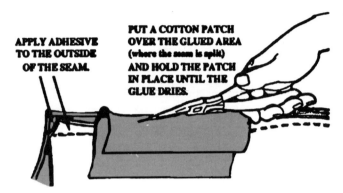

APPLY ADHESIVE TO THE OUTSIDE OF THE SEAM.

PUT A COTTON PATCH OVER THE GLUED AREA (where the seam is split) AND HOLD THE PATCH IN PLACE UNTIL THE GLUE DRIES.

Illustration #13

If the body is strong and is in good condition, remove a little of the stuffing. This tactic will make the repair faster and easier. Remove only as much of the stuffing that's needed. Slide a Kelly Forceps or a long nosed pliers along the seam on the inside of the body until it rests directly under the split seam (see illustration #13). Carefully apply glue to the open seam and coat both edges with adhesive. Use the forceps or pliers to grab the edges of the leather from the inside of the body. Do not use so much glue that the forceps get stuck. Clamp the forceps or close the pliers until the seam dries. Next, cut a cotton patch that is slightly larger than the repaired area. Saturate the cotton with adhesive and use a crochet hook or knitting needle to work it into place on the inside of the body, just over the split seam. When the patch begins to adhere to the inside to the body, carefully brush a coat of glue over the patch and extend it onto the surrounding leather. After the patch dries, work the stuffing back into place.

When doing a seam repair, check all of the other seams. Even if they appear to be weak, reinforce them now while the thread is still intact and the seam remains together. Use a mixture of 3/4ths glue to 1/4th water. Put the mixture in your applicator bottle. Place the tip of the applicator directly against the seam (see illustration #14). Squeeze the applicator and let the diluted glue run down into the seam below the stitches. Apply the adhesive mixture along the full length of the seam (from one end to the other). Wait a moment until the glue soaks into the deepest recesses of the seam, then go back and apply a second line of adhesive to the seam. Apply enough adhesive to saturate the seams below the

Illustration #14

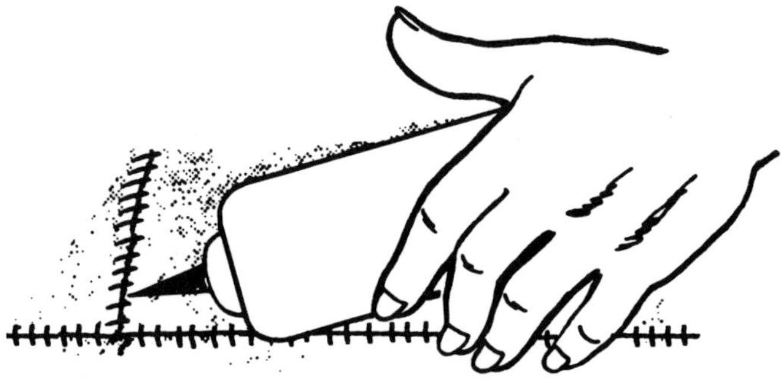

stitches. Shake the diluted glue frequently to keep it mixed. Repeat these steps as often as necessary. Soaking the seam with a coating of glue reduces the stress on the stitches and improves their strength. Wipe all excess glue from the body between each application.

Gusset Repair

Damaged gussets are repaired in much the same way as a split seam. Again, the method you select will depend on the condition of the body along with the location and the extent of the damage. When repairing gussets, always work a small area at a time. Since gussets are either round or oval, you must work around a curve and at an angle to make the repair. A small area is easier to handle.

When a gusset is damaged extensively, the work is usually faster and easier if you remove the stuffing before you make the repair. However, if you can reach the damaged area with your fingers, you will not have to remove the stuffing. Hold the cotton patch in place and keep the seam together with your fingers, a pliers, or a forceps.

If the repair involves one or two open stitches, drip glue in the opening and coat both edges of the leather with adhesive. Pinch the seam between your fingers to hold the edges together until the glue dries. Then reinforce the surrounding area with a mixture of glue and water as described in the previous section, *Repairing a Split Seam*.

Tears in the leather body adjoining the gusset are repaired in exactly the same way that any other rip is repaired. Cut a leather patch to follow the contour of the tear. Bevel the edges and apply the patch to the inside of the body. Refer to the section *Repairing a Split or Tear* for more details.

Repairing Pin-Jointed Bodies

Pin-jointed (universal) bodies are made from several separate sections that are assembled to complete the body. Therefore, they are easier to repair than a one piece gusset type body. When the leather of a pin jointed body is in good condition, removing the stuffing before you make the repair is the most practical approach. Damage to the leather, which is on the surface of the body, should be repaired after the limb is restuffed. For loose and split seams refer to the section *Repairing a Split Seam*.

The most common problem with pin-jointed bodies are holes in the leather under and around the buttons that join the legs and attach the limbs to the torso. These metal buttons have sharp edges that cut into the leather when the limbs move. Eventually the leather wears away and holes result.

To repair these holes, begin by removing the limbs. Check both sides of the limb to see which side has the least amount of damage. Slide a little piece of cardboard underneath the button on the side of the limb with the least amount of damage. Arrange the cardboard so that it is in contact with all of the sharp lower edges of the button. The cardboard keeps the button from cutting deeper into the leather when you remove the limb. Arrange the cardboard so that it is in contact with all of the sharp lower edges of the button.

The buttons are held in place with a piece of wire that is bent to form a hook. With the cardboard in place, push against the opposite side of the limb to compress it and force it up against the cardboard. There should now be enough slack between the button and the limb to let you straighten the wire and remove the button. After you remove the first button, pull the wire through the limb. Removing the wire detaches the limb from the body. Next, remove enough stuffing from the limb to enable you to reach inside the limb and touch the area around the button. Glue a leather patch to the inside of the limb at the point where the leather is damaged.

If the leather under the button is fragile and badly damaged, cut it away. Trim it to remove the jagged edges around the hole and then reconstruct it. Use the same method that you would use to mend a hole in the leather. Trim away the damaged leather, then glue a patch to the inside of the limb. Let the patch dry, then stuff the limb. Finally, apply a patch to the outside to fill the depression between the body and the patch. See the section on *Repairing Holes* for more detailed instruction.

Whenever possible, avoid sewing the leather to make the repair. Most old leather is fragile and unstable. Punching extra needle holes into leather that is already weak usually does more harm than good. When you must sew on unsound leather, line it first. There are three ways you can do this. The first way to line it is with iron-on interfacing. Another way is to iron a muslin liner to the leather using Fun Fuse® or Stitch Witchery® as the bonding agent. The last method is to use a clear drying flexible white glue to join a muslin liner to the leather. Extensively damaged leather remains delicate in spite of the lining, so handle it carefully. Make as few stitches as possible and do not pull them tight.

Repairing Cloth Lower Legs
(below & including the knee)

It's quite common to find cloth legs or cloth feet on old leather bodies. The fabric is usually soiled, weak, and leaking stuffing. There are 3 ways to make the repairs. You can repair the outside of the cloth legs, recover the legs or line the inside of the legs.

Repairs that are commonly needed to be done to the outside of the cloth include sizing fragile and/or stained cloth and covering tiny holes. Sizing a piece of fabric involves coating it with a glue mixture.

If the fabric is in good condition but has become fragile, size it to give it added strength. Brush on fabric stiffener, spray several applications of spray (laundry) starch, or brush on several applications of a sizing mixture. An easy sizing mixture to make is one package of unflavored Knox® brand gelatin thoroughly dissolved in 1 cup of hot water.

If the fabric is badly stained, plus needs to be sized, consider sizing them with a thin mixture of white glue, ivory or fawn colored water based paint, and water. Tint the glue to an off white color that resembles the color of the old fabric. Add water until it is the consistency of heavy cream. Apply with a soft sponge and let it dry completely between each application.

If there is a tiny hole in a cloth leg, it may be repaired with interfacing. Slip the interfacing through the hole to the inside of the leg and press it into place with a warm iron.

The second way to repair cloth legs is to recover them. To recover the legs, use either muslin or cotton fabric. Draft a pattern for the leg coverings from aluminum foil. Press it around the leg until it is smooth and conforms perfectly. Then, cut the foil at the seam lines of the old leg. Flatten the foil pattern. Place it on a piece of paper and trace the outline (the foil pattern) onto the paper. Add an 1/4th of an inch for the seam allowance. The pattern is now ready for use.

Cut the pattern pieces from the cotton or muslin fabric. Use a hot iron to press the seam allowance under. Place the covering on the leg and align it from top to bottom. Make certain the covering matches the leg at the centerfront. Use straight (common) pins to hold the covering in place against the leg. Work your way around the leg from front to back, smoothing the fabric as you go. Continue around the leg to the back seam. The fabric should be smooth, the points should match, and the covering must be held firmly in place with the pins. Adjust the seam allowance (which was previously pressed under) so it follows the seam at the back of the leg and lays perfectly flat. Use tiny stitches to hand sew the seams together. At the top, where the cloth meets the fabric, sew the covering to the top of the old fabric leg. Do not sew into the leather. Join the foot of the new fabric to the leg and then close the toe. Slip it onto the doll and make certain it fits snugly. If not, remove and adjust it.

Where you sew the recovered cloth leg to the leather body depends on the type of doll. For a gusseted body, the cloth leg is sewn to the leather just below the knee gusset. The leather and fabric join together to form one continuous piece. On a pin-jointed (universal) body the cloth leg is a separate piece — it does not attach to the leather. The cloth leg is wired to the body at the knee joint.

The third way to repair cloth legs is by lining them on the inside. The reason this method is appealing is that the old fabric remains exposed and the doll still looks old and untouched.

To repair a pin-jointed (universal) body by lining the inside of the legs, remove the legs according to the instructions given earlier in the section on *Repairing Pin-Jointed Bodies*. After removing the legs, examine them to determine where they were sewn closed. They were either sewn closed at the top of the knee or at the bottom (the sole) of the foot. Carefully open the hand sewn seam. Remove the stuffing and turn the legs inside out. Use a soft brush to brush away any traces of stuffing that cling to the inside of the legs.

If the fabric is soiled, wash it in warm water using a neutral soap. Soak the fabric and gently squeeze the suds through it. Do not rub and scrub. Rinse repeatedly in cool water until all traces of the soap are removed. When the legs become damp to dry, press them with a moderate iron until the fabric is completely dry and smooth.

Draw a pattern of the old leg on an index card or some type of lightweight cardboard. Use the pattern to cut the lining from cotton or muslin fabric. Also, cut 2 legs from a fusing material (Fun Fuse® or Stitch Witchery®). Place the fusing material against the inside of the old leg. Lay the new cloth leg on top of the fusing material. Adjust until both are perfectly aligned with the old leg. The fusing material is sandwiched between the old and new fabric. Bond the pieces together with an iron (set on the cotton setting). Hold the iron in place for 10 seconds and press it down. Let the fabric cool for a moment before you go on to the next area. Continue pressing until the old and new fabric bond.

Sew up your open seams. If the seam at the top of the leg or the bottom of the foot is open, reverse the leg and stuff it. Close the opening by hand sewing. If the leg is completely open, machine sew the seam at the back of the leg to close it. Leave an opening at either the top of the leg or the bottom of the foot so you can reverse the leg. Then, stuff the leg and finish closing the seam by hand. If the old fabric is extremely weak at the seam line, you may choose to close the seam by sewing a new seam line just inside the line of the old seam. If you prefer, you may open the entire seam along the back of the leg as well as the one at the top of the leg and bottom of the foot. This way the old legs will lay perfectly flat while you work on them.

Lining the lower legs on a gusseted body is a bit more difficult than working with the legs of a pin-jointed body. The legs remain attached to the body during the repair so you must contend with the body's bulk while you are working. First, examine the feet to see how they were assembled. If the seam at the back of the leg runs down the leg and through the center of the sole of the foot in one continuous seam, the easiest method is to open the entire seam — including the seam in the sole of the foot. If there is a seam at the outer edge of the foot and not one through the sole, the top of the foot and the sole were sewn together first, before they were sewn to the lower leg. In this instance, open the seam in the back of the leg (only). Begin at the top of the leg where the fabric is sewn to the leather. Open the seam from that point all the way to the heel.

To remove the stuffing, work through the open seam at the back of the leg. Take a small amount out of the leather too, just up to the lower edge of the knee gusset. Pack the lower edges of the knee gussets with a little cotton to keep the remaining stuffing in place while you work.

Turn the feet inside out and line them with a fusing material and cotton or muslin, as described earlier. Begin by bonding the new fabric to the toe and upper foot area of the old body. Then, bond tiny new soles to the bottoms of the old feet. Next, line the leg. When you cut the fusing material and fabric to line the remainder of the leg, allow an extra 1/4th of an inch, or even slightly more, at the top of the leg. This forms a bond over the seam where the cloth lower leg joins the leather. Begin bonding at the top, centerfront of the leg. Work on only one half (one side) of the leg at a time. Begin at the top and work down the side of the leg. Stop just slightly above the ankle. Repeat this for the other side of the leg. Finish the reinforcement by bonding the area around the ankle last.

Hand stitch the seams to close. Begin at the top of the leg, near the knee. Close the seam halfway down the leg. Remove the cotton from the knee gusset and replace the stuffing in the gusset. Then, stuff the remainder of the leg. You must alternate between hand stitching the seam and filling the leg with stuffing until the leg is refilled and the seam is closed.

Illustration #15

There is an alternate method that you may prefer to use if you don't mind an extra bit of hand sewing. Open the seam along the back of the leg and also the seam that is holding the sole of the foot in place (see illustration #15). With the back leg seam open and the sole of the foot removed, the fabric in the lower leg will lie flat while you work.

Do not remove the legs from the body where they join the leather.

Although this may seem to make the repair easier to accomplish, reattaching the cloth lower limbs to weak leather is a nightmare. Lining the inside of the attached legs is a slow process for it requires a good deal of time and patience. Yet, attaching the cloth to the leather portion of the leg requires even more time. I've found it is best not to remove the legs of a gusseted body.

Enlarging & Reducing the Pattern

Regardless of the method you select to enlarge or reduce your pattern, I want to caution you to honor all copyrights. Failure to do so is in direct violation of the law and you could find yourself facing legal action. If you buy a pattern that is copyrighted, you have the right to use that pattern for your own use, but you do not have the right to enlarge or reduce it and then reproduce it for resale, or the like. Before you reproduce a pattern, look for a copyright. If the pattern is in a book or magazine, check to see if the author has released the pattern, or given the purchaser of the book or magazine permission to reproduce the pattern. Usually, they have. Of course, you have the right to enlarge or reduce the patterns in this book for your own personal use, only.

There are several inexpensive ways to enlarge and reduce a pattern. One method is to use a pantograph. This is a series of jointed wooden arms, reminiscent of the old fashioned expansion type hat racks. They are fairly inexpensive and available through most fabric centers and office supply shops. The pantograph can enlarge or reduce by adjusting the screws. The screws also act as the joints. One end of the pantograph is clamped to the work table. The right hand operates the tracer while the left hand holds the pencil that either reduces or enlarges the pattern. There is no need to go into further detail here; complete instructions for the adjustment and operation are provided with the pantograph when you purchase one.

Inexpensive projectors designed to enlarge drawings and photos are available through most office supply and art stores. These projectors, made of plastic, are designed to throw the enlarged image against a wall. They consist of nothing more than a series of mirrors and an electric light bulb that pick up and reflect the image through an enlarging lens in the front of the machine. The size of the enlargement is controlled by moving the lens. These must be used in a darkened room if the image is to be sharp and clear.

If you do not wish to invest in another piece of equipment or take the time to reproduce the pattern yourself, have it enlarged or reduced on a photocopier. Copiers can make almost any size enlargement or reduction within seconds. Take the pattern to your office supply store, print shop, or place of business where copiers are sold. Almost every small town has at least one or two places where copiers are made available for the public.

Remember to check and honor the copyright!

Pin-Jointed Bodies

General Information About
Pin-Jointed Bodies

To save time follow the instructions exactly, in the order given. By following the instructions, it is possible to make an entire body in the time that is ordinarily required to baste a body.

The first pieces that are basted or glued are the first pieces to be machine sewn. The seam allowance is 1/8 inch. Apply the glue sparingly to the seam allowance. Do not allow adhesive to extend beyond the seam allowance. After gluing, press the seams firmly together. Begin at the inner edge and push toward the outer (cut) edge to force the excess out, through the seam. Use paper clips to hold the pieces together until the glue dries (see the illustration at the right). Place the tip of the paper clip at the edge of the leather so it contacts the glued area only. Use care when removing paper clips to avoid damaging the leather. Tie and glue the ends of all loose threads after machine sewing.

Use Paper Clips to Dry the Adhesive

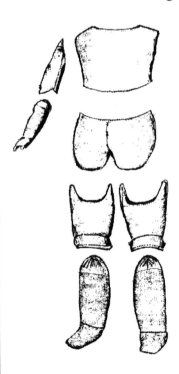

Unassembled Body

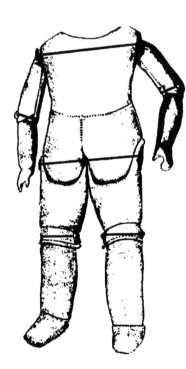

Location of Wires

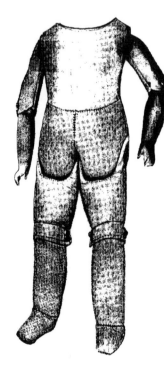

Assembled Body

Instructions for Glue Assembly of Pin-Jointed Bodies

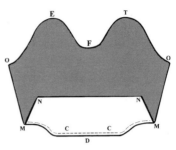

#1. Join Upper Leg and Knee Facing

With right (smooth) sides together, glue the knee facing to the bottom edge of the upper leg.
Match points M, C and D.
Carefully ease the leather between points M and C.
Repeat for the other leg.

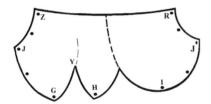

#2. Lower Body

With right sides together, apply glue to close the edge of the seam from points G to Y to point H. Repeat for the other lower body section. Ease between pieces as necessary.

#3. Join Front and Back Torso

With right sides together, glue the front and back pieces of the torso together at the side seams. Match and glue from points Q to P.

#4. Close Side Seams of Upper Arms

With right (smooth) sides together, glue the side seams of the upper arms from point K to L.

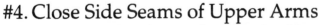

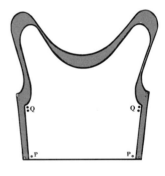

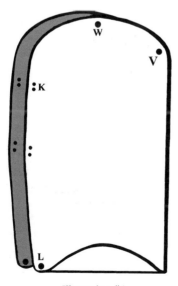

#5. Join Upper Leg and Knee Facing

Machine stitch (along the lower edge where it was previously glued) the knee facing to the upper leg. Sew from point M through D to M. Allow 1/8th inch for the seam. Repeat for the other leg.

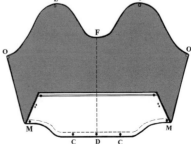

#6. Lower Body

Machine stitch point G/H to Y. Continue along Y to the end of the dash line, sewing in one uninterrupted seam. Repeat for the other leg.

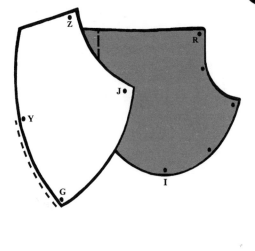

Illustration #6

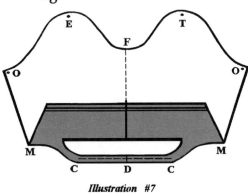

Illustration #7

#7. Join Leather Knee Facing and Cardboard Liner

Glue the cardboard knee liner into position on the wrong (rough side) of the knee facing. Position the liner 1/16th of an inch from the seam line. If necessary, trim the edges of the cardboard to follow the curve of the seam. Repeat for the other leg.

#8. Leather Knee Facing

After the cardboard liner is in position turn the knee facing under, along the seam line, at the lower edge of the leg. Adjust and smooth it so the seam line is just slightly toward the inside of the leg. Repeat for the other leg.

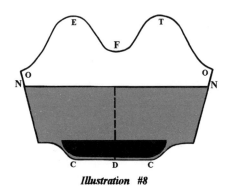

Illustration #8

Illustration #9

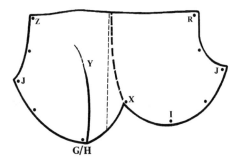

#9. Lower Body

With right sides together, match and glue from point G/H to point I . Glue along the seam from that point to point X. Hold in place with paper clips. Repeat for the other lower body section. After the glue dries, machine sew from point G/H and I to point X . Continue sewing from X, along the dash line, in one continuous seam.

#10. Muslin (Torso) Liner

Glue the muslin torso liner to the rough side of the leather torso. Center one piece of the muslin liner on the torso. Keep the lower edge of the leather torso (point P to P) even with the edge of the liner. Glue the liner and torso together along the side seams (only) from Q to P. Trim the excess muslin along the side seams but do not trim past point Q. Next, turn the torso over. With the muslin liner down and the opposite (rough) side of the leather torso up, place the liner over the leather. Adjust as directed earlier. Glue the liner into position along the side seams from Q to P.

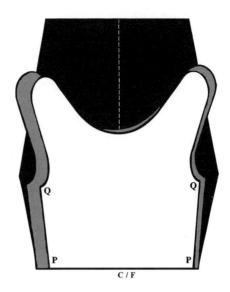

Illustration #10

#11. Upper Arms

Machine sew a leather upper arm from point K to L. Refer to illustration #4. Repeat for the other arm.

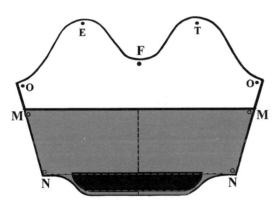

Illustration #12

#12. Top Stitch Cardboard Liner to Upper Leg

Machine sew through the cardboard liner in the upper leg. Top stitch 1/4th inch from the lower edge of the leg. Use the lower edge of the leg as a seam guide. Stitch in a straight line. Repeat for the other leg.

#13. Join the Back of the Upper Leg

Match and glue the seam at the back of the leg together. Begin at point N (the bottom edge of the knee facing) and work through point M (the seam between leg and knee facing) and O at the top of the leg. Repeat for the other leg.

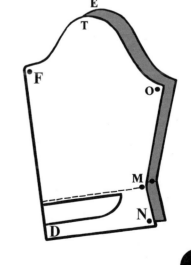

Illustration #13

#14. Lower Body

With right sides together, glue to join point J to point J. Then begin at the joined points (J) and apply glue, working toward point G/H/I. Match the dots and ease the leather as necessary to follow the curve. Repeat for the other section of the lower body. Refer to illustration 19 for finished pieces.

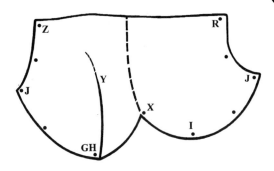

Illustration #14

#15. Upper Arms

Turn the arms right (smooth) side out. Turn the top (upper portion) of the arm down and fold it over the bottom (lower portion) of the arm. Insert the cardboard liner into the lower portion of the arm (see illustration #15A). Match the edge of the cardboard to the seam. One edge of the cardboard liner should touch but not cover the seam in the arm. Shape the liner so it circles the arm. The remaining edge of the cardboard should also come up to but not extend over the seam. If necessary, adjust and trim the cardboard. Place the cardboard liner 1/8th inch from the edge of the leather and glue it into place (see illustration #15B). Clip the curved area (leather) at the bottom of the arm. Do not cut it out. Glue the leather allowance of 1/8th inch up, inside of the arm, against the cardboard liner.

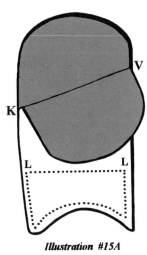

Illustration #15A

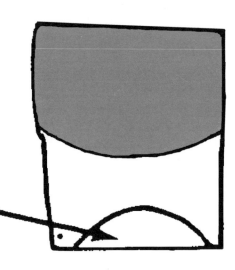

Illustration #15B

#16. Machine Sew Upper Legs

Machine sew the seam at the back of the upper legs. Begin at point O and sew through points M and N (the knee facing) in one continuous seam. Repeat for the other leg.

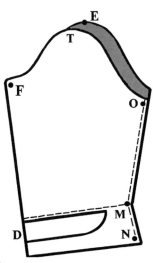

Illustration #16

#17. Glue Oval Leather Leg Facing to Upper Legs

Slash the top of the oval leather upper leg facing along the line as indicated on the pattern. With the right sides together, position the oval knee facing at the top edge of the leg. Match points 1, F, E, and 0. Glue the oval facing into position at those points only, matching the dots. Hold in place with paperclips. Do not attempt to glue the rest of the facing into place at this time. That portion of the work is completed after the glued points dry.

Illustration #18

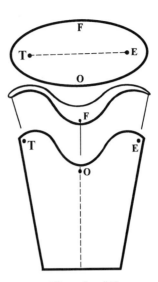

Illustration #17

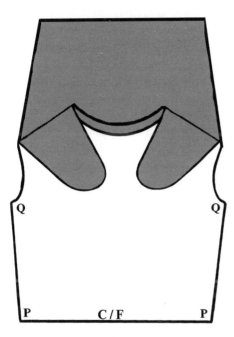

#18. Close the Side Seams of the Torso

Machine sew from points P to Q. When you reach point Q, stop but do not remove the needle from the torso. Turn the leather shoulder tabs toward the body. Then sew from point Q through the side seams of the muslin liner, to the top. This will be one continuous seam.

#19. Machine Sew the Lower Body

Begin at point J and sew through point G/H/ I. Continue sewing along the dash line to point X. Repeat for the other section of body. Refer to illustration 14.

#20. Glue the Two Lower Body Sections

Place the lower body sections together with the right (smooth) sides facing. To do this, turn one piece inside out. Turn the remaining piece right (smooth) side out. Place one piece inside the other and fit them together. Match point R to R, J to J, and O to O. Keep the crotch seam matched. Glue and ease as necessary. Hold the pieces in place with paperclips.

Illustration #20

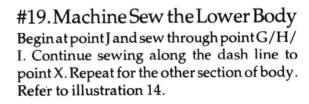

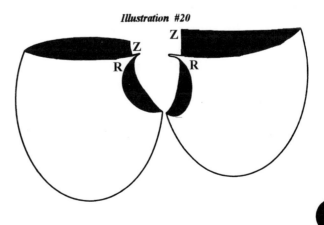

#21. Upper Leg Facing

Glue the oval upper leg facing into place against the upper leg. Refer to the steps in #17. Glue between point T to A. Ease as necessary and hold in place with paperclips. Continue around the oval knee facing from F to T, from T to O and from O back to E. Ease between each point. Secure with clips where needed. Repeat for the other leg.

Illustration #22

#22. Muslin Arm Liner

Machine sew the long seam of the muslin arm liner. Run a gathering thread along the bottom (lower) edge of the liner. Turn the liner right side out. Place the liner inside the leather arm. Position the seam of the liner against the seam of the arm. The lower edge of the liner should be even with the curved portion of the leather arm. Machine stitch the liner and leather together from point K, around the curved upper arm to the "V" in the leather. Trim off any excess muslin liner at the top of the arm. Finish the curved edge at the top of the arm with a whip stitch. Pad the upper portion of the arm with a little cotton. Insert the cotton through the lower portion of the arm. Stuff the remainder of the arm. Close by pulling drawstrings and tie them securely. Secure the knot with a drop of glue.

#23. Machine Sew the Two Lower Body Sections

With the right (smooth) sides facing each other, stitch the lower body sections together from point O through points J and R.

Illustration #23

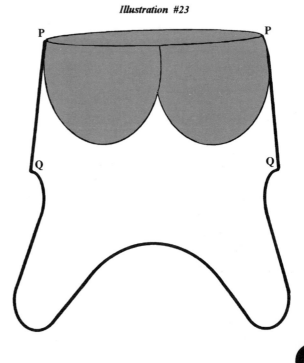

#24. Glue the Torso and Lower Body

Join the torso to the lower body with glue. Glue the leather only. Do not glue the muslin liner. With the right (smooth) sides facing each other, match the side seams and centerpoints. Glue and secure them with paperclips. Next, glue and ease the leather between the four points. Again, secure the leather with paperclips. (There is not an accompanying illustration for this step.)

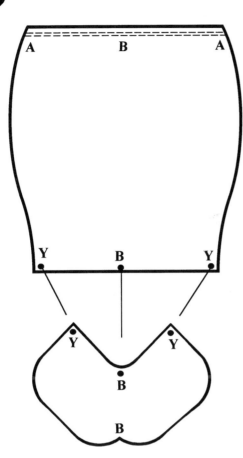

#25. Muslin Lower Leg

With right sides together, join the foot to the lower leg. Match the centerfront of the leg at point B. Match points Y. Baste and then machine stitch. Repeat for the other leg. With right sides together baste back leg seams together. Begin at point A. Match notches and cross seams. Baste from A to Y at the back of the leg. Continue from Y to B (at the toe). Machine stitch. Repeat for other leg. Run two rows of gathering stitches at the top of each leg. Stuff the legs firmly. Draw the gathering strings together tightly to close the tops. Invert the raw edge of the fabric. Tie securely.

Illustration #25B

Illustration #25A

#26. Machine Sew the Upper Leg to Upper Leg Facing

Sew the oval upper leg facing to the upper leg. (There is not an accompanying illustration.)

#27. Add Cardboard Liner to Upper Leg Facing

Place the oval cardboard liner inside the upper leg. The cardboard liner should be slightly larger than the leather (oval) facing. The seam that joins the leather facing to the upper leg should be on or just slightly over the top off the cardboard liner. After inserting the cardboard liner adjust the opening (slash) in the leather so that the edges meet. Then glue the liner into place against the upper leg facing.

Illustration #27

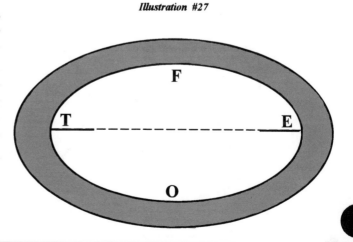

#28. Stuff the Upper Legs

Work through the opening at the bottom of the leg. Place a little cotton in each side of the oval facing. Pull the loose portion of the knee facing up, to the outside of the leg. Stuff and pack the remainder of the leg with sawdust or ground cork. Place a thin layer of cotton over the stuffing. Trim the liner so that it reaches the center of the leg opening and covers the stuffing. Close the liner with glue.

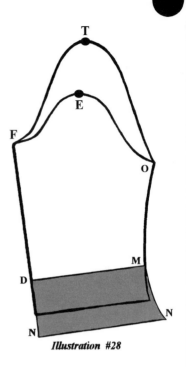

Illustration #28

#29. Sew Torso to Lower Body

Machine sew the torso and lower body together at the waistline. Include the muslin liner in this stitching. Refer to illustration #23.

#30. Stuff the Body

Refer to page 11.

#31. Close the Top of the Muslin Liner

Trim the muslin liner, allowing an 1/2 inch seam allowance. Turn the seam allowance under, to the inside. Pull both edges of the muslin liner as tightly as possible. Allow a slight overlap between the two pieces. Whip stitch along the top edge to close the liner (see illustration #31A). Fold the side up, toward the center of the body (see illustration #31B). Pull up as tightly as possible and whip stitch.

Illustration #31A

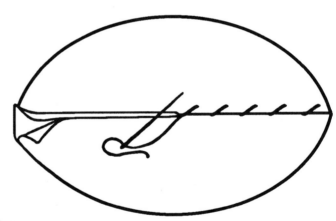

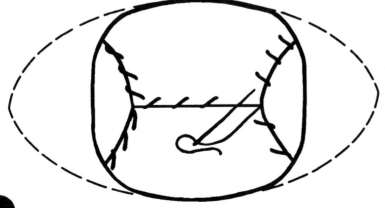

Illustration #31B

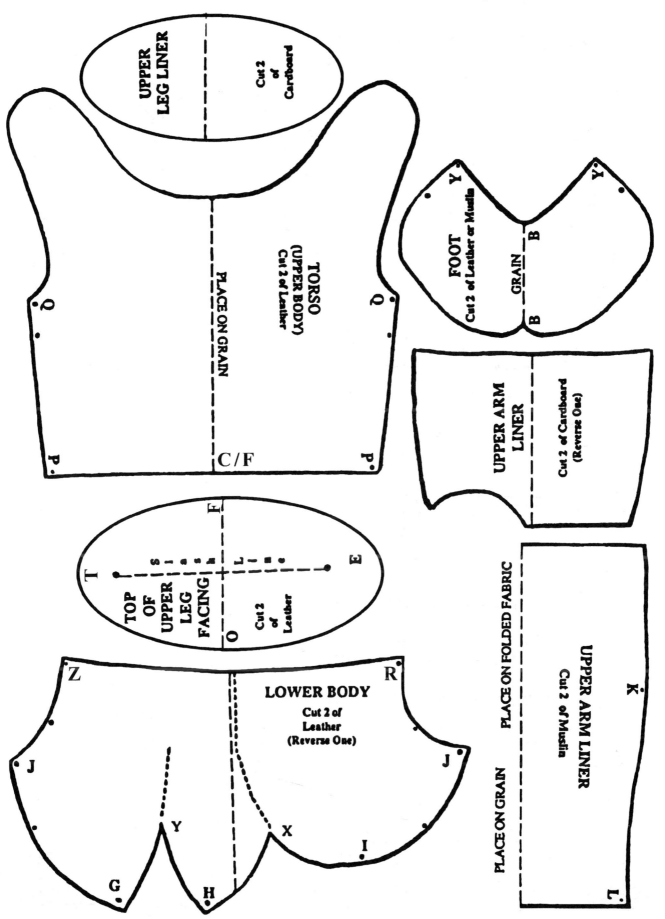

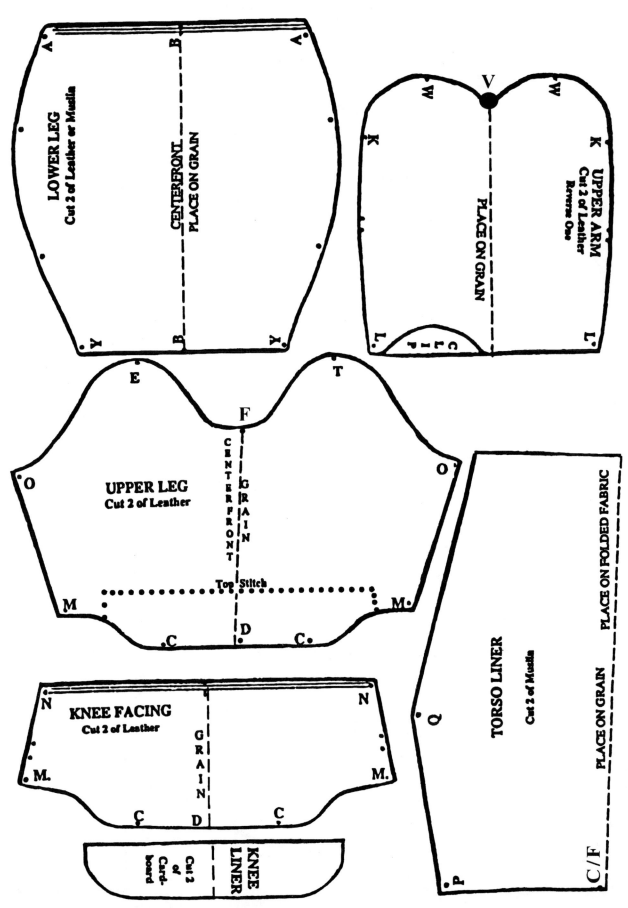

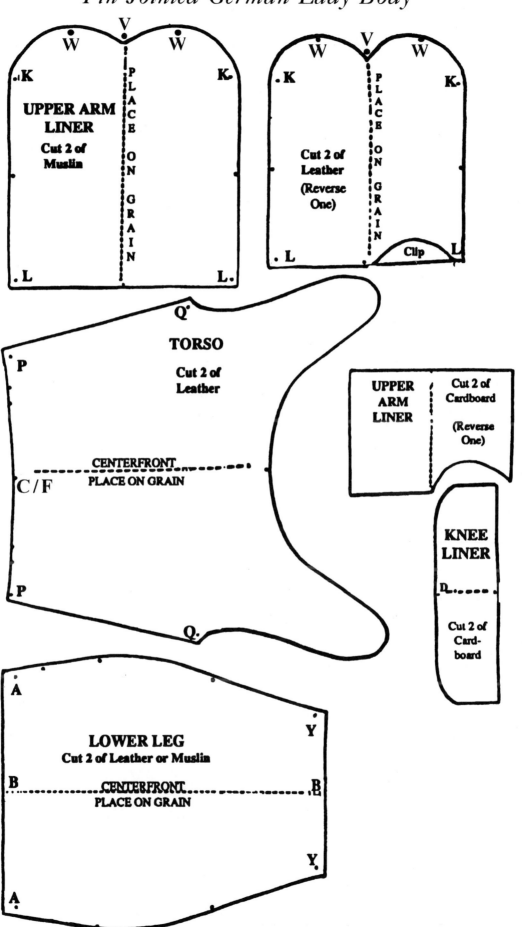

UPPER ARM LINER

Cut 2 of Muslin

PLACE ON GRAIN

Cut 2 of Leather (Reverse One)

PLACE ON GRAIN

Clip

TORSO

Cut 2 of Leather

CENTERFRONT

C / F

PLACE ON GRAIN

UPPER ARM LINER

Cut 2 of Cardboard

(Reverse One)

KNEE LINER

Cut 2 of Cardboard

LOWER LEG

Cut 2 of Leather or Muslin

CENTERFRONT

PLACE ON GRAIN

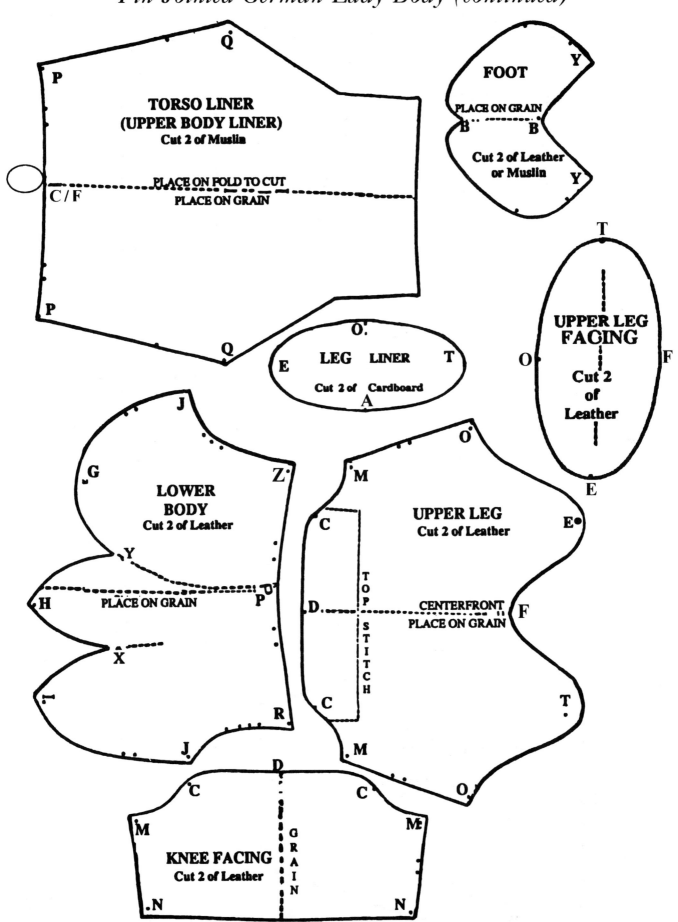

Gusset Bodies

Assembly Instructions for a Full Gusset Body
Leather Over Shoulderplate

1. With right (smooth) sides together, join the foot to the lower leg. Match the centerfront T and the side points H. Glue it and let it dry. Then machine stitch it. Repeat for the other foot.

2. Baste or glue the knee gussets in place on the upper leg. Match the centerpoints J and the side points B. Ease between points until the gusset fits. Machine sew. Repeat for the other leg.

3. With right (smooth) sides together (facing), join the upper and lower leg section. Match centerpoint M and sidepoints L. Glue. and machine stitch. Repeat for the other leg.

4. With the right sides together (facing), gently fold the leg on the centerline. Baste or glue the leg from point G through point R to point N. Begin again at point P and baste or glue through the points P, L, and H. Continue around the foot to point S. Machine sew. To close the toe, machine sew from the centerline to point S. Repeat for the other leg.

5. Baste or glue the hip gusset into place in the upper leg. Match points N, 0, P, and 0. Ease between the points. Machine stitch. Repeat for the other leg.

6. To close the crotch, turn one leg right side out. Place it against the other (unturned) leg so that the right (smooth) sides of the leather are facing. Baste or glue the two pieces together at the crotch by matching point F to point C/F. Machine sew the crotch closed. When complete, turn both legs right side out.

7. Place the leather torso pieces together with the right (smooth) sides facing Baste or glue the side seams from point J to point F. Note: The back will be slightly smaller than the front.

8. With the back of the muslin liner facing you, glue the back torso liner into place along the edge of the side seams. Adjust the liner so that it is evenly centered. Baste or glue as close to the outer edge of the seam line as possible. Trim muslin liner if necessary .

9. Turn the torso over so that the rough side of the leather is facing you. Glue or baste the front torso liner to the front leather torso. Work as close to the edge of the leather as possible.

10. Machine sew the side seams of the torso. Begin at point F and sew to point J. When you reach point J, stop but do not remove the torso from the machine. Turn the leather shoulder tab toward the inside of the body so that you will not stitch into them. Continue to sew from point J through the side of the muslin liner, to the neck. Repeat for the other side of the seam. Do not sew the lower edge of the liner to the lower edge of the torso at this time. Do not turn the torso right side out.

11. Place the lower body into the torso. The right (smooth) sides of the lower body will be facing you. Slide the lower body into the torso through the neck opening of the torso. Make certain that the front of the torso and the front of the body are together. Match the side points F and the centerpoints at the waist. Machine sew. Turn torso right side out.

12. Baste or glue the elbow gusset into place on the upper arm. Match points Z and Y. Ease between points. Machine stitch. Repeat for the other arm.

13. Close the side seam of the upper arm. Baste or glue and then machine sew from points X to V. Repeat for the other arm.

14. Glue bisque lower arms into place on the leather upper arms. Let them dry. Stuff the arms 3/4ths of the way to the top of the arm. Set the arms at the proper length on the body. Stitch the upper arms into place against the muslin liner.

NOTE PATTERN VARIATIONS: If the lower leg is to be made of cloth, the seam between the upper and lower leg is necessary. It is the point where the leather and fabric are joined. If the lower leg is to be made of leather, align the pattern pieces to eliminate this seam when you cut it out. When cutting cloth lower legs, add 1/8th inch to the outer edge of the pattern. This will allow for a slightly deeper (1/4th inch) seam in the areas where cloth is being used. This pattern is designed for leather, so no seam width adjustment is necessary when making leather lower legs. The usual seam allowance of 1/8th inch for leather will be used throughout the entire construction.

Full Gusset Body Pattern

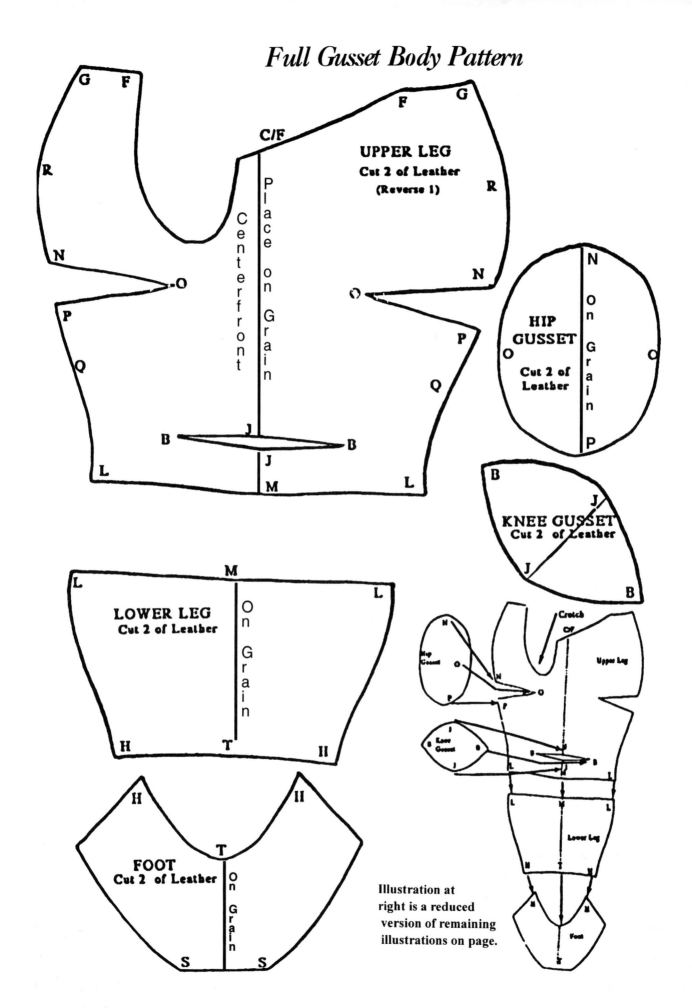

UPPER LEG
Cut 2 of Leather
(Reverse 1)

Centerfront

Place on Grain

HIP GUSSET
Cut 2 of Leather

On Grain

KNEE GUSSET
Cut 2 of Leather

LOWER LEG
Cut 2 of Leather

On Grain

FOOT
Cut 2 of Leather

On Grain

Illustration at
right is a reduced
version of remaining
illustrations on page.

Full Gusset Body Pattern (continued)

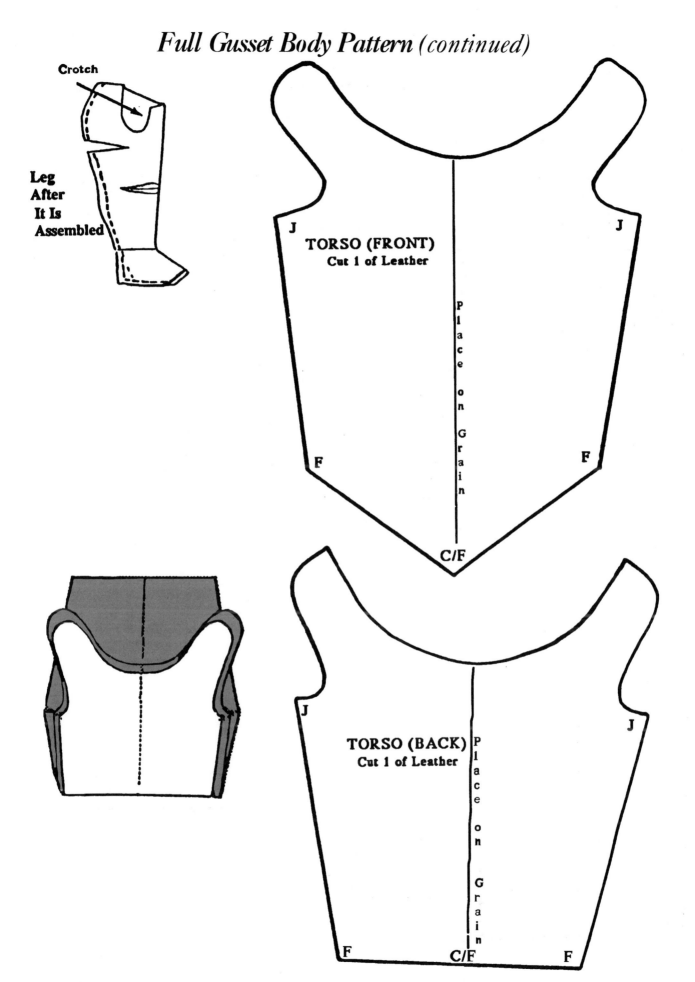

Crotch

Leg After It Is Assembled

TORSO (FRONT)
Cut 1 of Leather

J   J

Place on Grain

F   F

C/F

TORSO (BACK)
Cut 1 of Leather

J   J

Place on Grain

F   C/F   F

Full Gusset Body Pattern (continued)

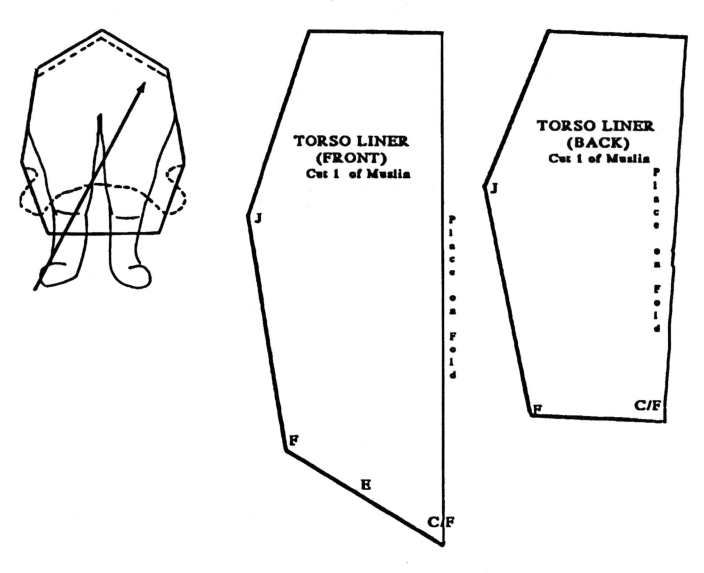

TORSO LINER (FRONT)
Cut 1 of Muslin

Place on Fold

J

F

E

C/F

TORSO LINER (BACK)
Cut 1 of Muslin

Place on Fold

J

F

C/F

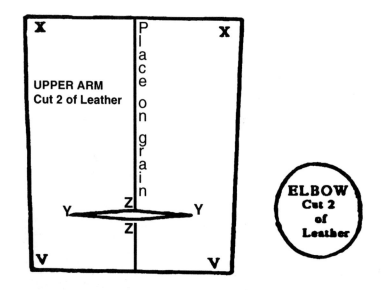

UPPER ARM
Cut 2 of Leather

X   X

Place on grain

Z

Y   Y

Z

V   V

ELBOW
Cut 2
of
Leather

Assembly Instructions for Full Gusset Body
Bisque Shoulderplate Over Leather

1. With right (smooth) sides together join the foot to the lower leg Match centerfront. points S and side points A. Glue or baste . When the glue dries, machine stitch. Repeat for the other foot.

2. Baste or glue the knee gusset into place on the upper leg. Match centerpoints J and side points B. Ease between the points until the gusset fits. Machine sew. Repeat for the other leg.

3. With right (smooth) sides together (facing), join the upper and lower leg section. Match points L, M, and L. Baste or glue. Machine stitch. Repeat for the other leg

4. With right sides together (facing), gently fold the leg on the centerline. Baste or glue the leg from point G through R to N. Begin again at point P and baste or glue from P through the points P, L, and H. Machine sew. To close the leg and finish the foot, baste the sole into place, matching points. Machine sew. Repeat for the other leg

5. Baste or glue the hip gusset into place on the upper leg. Match points N, O, P, and 0. Ease between points. Machine stitch. Repeat for the other leg.

6. To close the crotch, turn one leg right side out. Place the leg against the other (unturned) leg so the right (smooth) sides of the leather are together. Baste or glue the two pieces together at the crotch by matching points F and C / F. Machine sew to close the crotch. When sewing is completed, turn both legs right side out.

7. Place the front and back pieces of the leather torso together with the right (smooth) sides facing. Baste or glue the side seams from point F to J to K Note: The back will be slightly smaller than the front.

8. Line the back half of the leather torso. Place the back of the muslin torso liner on the back of the leather (rough side out) torso. Adjust the liner so that it is evenly centered on the leather torso. Baste or glue one side, from point F through J to K. Work as close to the outer edge of the seam as possible. Do not glue or baste the lower edge of the liner to the lower edge of the torso. Repeat for the other side. Trim the muslin liner if necessary.

9. Turn the torso over. With the rough side of the leather facing you, glue or baste the front torso liner to the front of the leather torso from point F to J. Do not glue or baste

the lower edge of the liner to the lower edge of the torso. Work as close to the edge of the leather as possible. Repeat for the other side. Trim the muslin liner if necessary.

10. Machine sew the side seams of the torso and liner together. See the illustration on page 31. Begin at point F and sew through points J to K When you reach point K, pull the leather out of the way so that you do not stitch through it . Continue sewing from point K to Z to close the remaining side seam of the muslin liner. Do not close the neck opening. Do not sew the lower edge of the liner to the lower edge of the torso at this time. Repeat for the other side seam. Do not turn the torso right side out after you finish sewing.

11. Join the lower body and the torso. *See the illustration on page 32.* Place the lower body into the torso. With the right (smooth) side of the lower body facing you, slide the lower body into the torso through the neck opening The torso front and body front must be together. Match the side points (F) and the centerpoints around the waist. Machine sew. Turn the torso right side out.

12. Close the side seam of the upper arm. Match points X and Z. Match points Z and V. Baste or glue. Machine sew. Repeat for the other arm.

13. Baste or glue the elbow gusset into place in the upper arm. Match points Z and Y. Ease between the points. Machine stitch. Repeat for the other arm.

14. Glue the bisque lower arms into place on the leather upper arms. Let them dry.

15. Stuff the arms 3/4ths of the way. Do not stuff the remaining 1/4th at the top of the arm.

16. Stuff the body.

17. Adjust the arms to the proper length on the body and stitch them into place against the muslin liner.

Full Gusset German Body

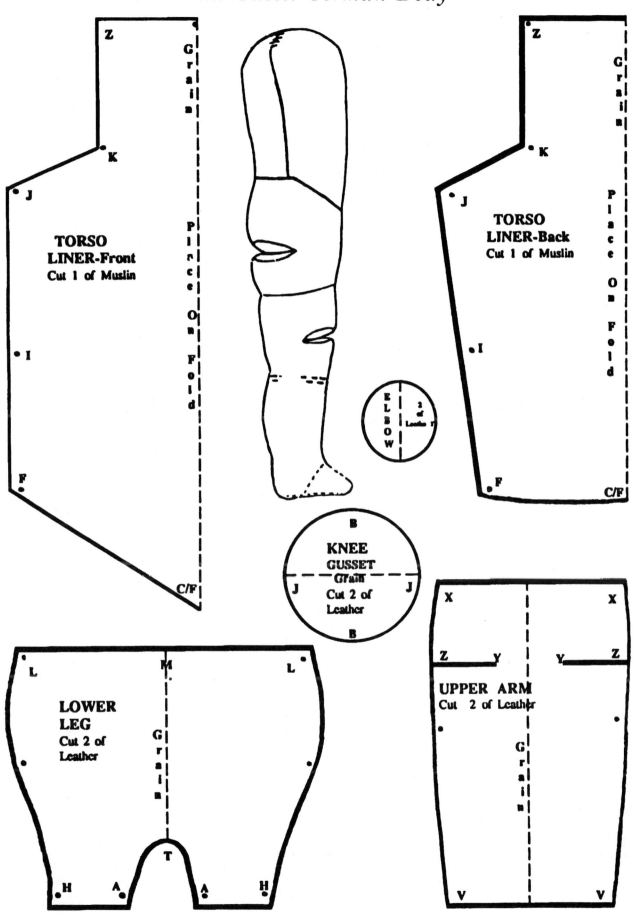

TORSO LINER-Front
Cut 1 of Muslin

Z

Grain

K

J

Place On Fold

I

F

C/F

TORSO LINER-Back
Cut 1 of Muslin

Z

Grain

K

J

Place On Fold

I

F

C/F

ELBOW
2 of Leather

KNEE GUSSET
Grain
J   J
Cut 2 of Leather
B
B

LOWER LEG
Cut 2 of Leather

L   M   L

Grain

H   A   T   A   H

UPPER ARM
Cut 2 of Leather

X   X

Z   Y   Y   Z

Grain

V   V

Full Gusset German Body

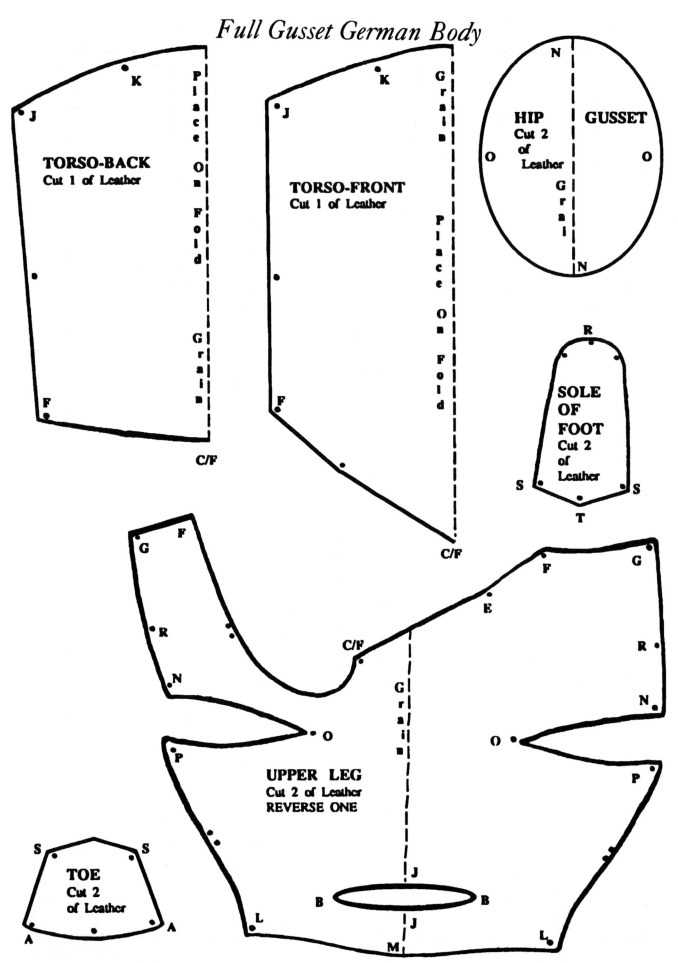

Notes

Notes

NEW!

TRACEABLE FACES FOR CLOTH DOLLS

BY BARB SPENCER

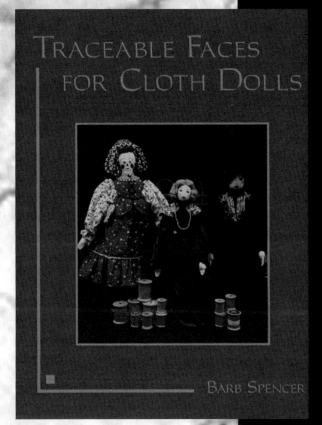

One of America's Foremost Cloth Doll Designers Shows Her Hints For Making Your Own Dream Doll Faces!

Barb Spencer has created the all-purpose guide to creating perfect cloth doll faces. She takes you—clearly and easily—from the preparation stages through to the details of finishing the face.

This guide gives you over 40 pages of traceable doll faces, most of which have never been shared before. And for the more creative dollmaker, Barb has included 80 "mix and match" facial features that enable you to create your very own dream doll faces. This book is a necessity for every cloth doll designer who wants his or her doll to radiate the love that went into making it.

ABOUT THE AUTHOR

Barb Spencer is one of America's foremost cloth doll designers, particularly celebrated for her doll faces. Her original designs have been shown in international markets, national advertising, and dollmaking classes. Along with owning her own shop, Barb also writes a column ("Hints From the Attic") for **Dollmaking** magazine.

This book will be your continuous source of inspiration for dollmaking. Buy it now—you will find endless possibilities for designing and producing your very own dolls!

Order Form

How To Make & Repair Leather Doll Bodies

Telephone Order: Call 1-800-331-0038 and have your Mastercard, Visa, AMEX or Discover ready. Please mention code "10623."

Fax Orders: Complete this form and fax it to 715-445-4053.

Mail Orders: Mail this form, along with your check (unless paying by credit card), to: Jones Publishing
Book Orders, Dept. 10623
P.O. Box 5000
Iola, WI 54945

Address:

Company Name: _____

Name: _____

Address: _____

City:_____ State: _____ Zip:_____

Quantity	Title	Unit Price	Total
_____	*How To Make & Repair Leather Doll Bodies*	$14.95	$_____
	Subtotal		$_____
	5.5% Sales Tax (Wisconsin residents only)		$_____
	Shipping (per book): $3.00 U.S., $5.00 Foreign		$_____
	TOTAL		$_____

Payment:

❏ Check (U.S. Funds)

❏ Visa   ❏ Mastercard   ❏ AMEX

Card Number: _____ Exp. Date:_____

Name on Card:_____

Signature:_____